Buffalo Jones
Citizen of the Kansas Frontier

by Phillip Drennon Thomas

Finney County Historical Society
Garden City, Kansas

Author Information:
Phillip Drennon Thomas is a Professor of History at Wichita State University and former dean of the colleges of arts and sciences at the universities of Alaska, Anchorage and Wichita State University. A co-author of the *Forest in American History*, his research interests focus upon the science, art, and natural history of the American West in the nineteenth century.

About the Artist Jerry Thomas:
Jerry D. Thomas is a Scott City, Kansas native, currently a resident of Manhattan, Kansas. Thomas has made a career of creating wildlife and western art. His original work appears on the covers of the Kansas Forts Series sponsored by the Kansas State Historical Society.

Buffalo Jones
Citizen of the Kansas Frontier

Copyright © 2004 Finney County Historical Society,

Library of Congress Control Number 2004112563
ISBN 0-9654410-8-3

Graphic Design & Book Layout by Larry G. Nichols II
Printed in the U.S.A. by Mennonite Press, Inc., Newton, KS

CONTENTS

INTRODUCTION

Charles Jesse Jones was a frontier entrepreneur whose diverse career and wanderings allowed him to become a hide hunter, an early promoter of Garden City, Kansas, a builder of irrigation ditches, an inventor of irrigation technology, a cross breeder of bison and cattle, a participant in both the race to settle lands on the Ute reservation in Colorado and the Cherokee Strip land rush in 1893[1], game warden at Yellowstone National Park, and a lecturer on African wildlife. While his role in preserving the bison is debated, he was acknowledged by George Bird Grinnell for having captured remnants of the southern herd and beginning a captive breeding program. Jones' exploits were described by Emerson Hough and Zane Grey and chronicled by many of the nation's leading newspapers. He was a frontier Odysseus whose wanderings and adventures assumed mythic proportions in the public's mind.

The life of Charles Jesse Jones is poorly recorded. Those who seek to reconstruct his life do so by depending upon Colonel Henry Inman's 1899 publication. Inman does not claim to be the author of the work, but rather the compiler of *Buffalo Jones' Forty Years of Adventure*. "A volume of facts gathered from experience, by Hon. C. J. Jones, whose eventful life has been devoted to the preservation of the American bison and other wild animals, who survived the perils of frozen north, the land of midnight sun, among Eskimos, Indians, and the ferocious beasts of North America[2]," this work is the primary source of information about Jones' career[3]. Few individuals have had a career that rival in interest, scope, and adventure that of Buffalo Jones. Yet his birth and early years bore no portent of the fame that would ultimately be his as he sought his elusive fortune in the West. Seldom satisfied with what he had, and always seeking the wealth which his latest ideas promised, he spent his life in quest of his elusive destiny. He found fame but not fortune.

Many of the details of his life are imperfectly known and the stories told about him, and by him, approach that of a frontier hagiography. There is no doubt that he would at times exaggerate his accomplishments with a frontier bravado that would equal that of other western heroes whose accomplishments were chronicled in the dime novels and popular literature of the era.

FREDERIC REMINGTON SKETCH OF BUFFALO JONES.

Yet, always beneath these tales is a solid level of accomplishment and experience that reflect his acquisition of frontier skills, his profound knowledge of western wildlife, his commitment to the growth and development of southwest Kansas and Garden City, and his desire to advance himself through his remarkable energy and entrepreneurial ambitions.

He was a settler, speculator, and dreamer. Many of his peers lacking the drive and imagination that he possessed were critical of the many ventures which he organized, promoted, and participated in. He was a frontier entrepreneur willing to take risks to win rewards. He expressed his philosophy on participating in speculative ventures when "being remonstrated with his recklessness in becoming involved in some six or eight of these affairs (establishment of county seats), justified his course by saying that he could afford to lose in all of them but one; that if in any single instance the town which he was backing became the county seat he and his associates would not only from their profits be able to recoup their losses in all their unsuccessful efforts, but would have enough left to make them independent for life."[4] Throughout his life the capital which he never lost was energy, imagination, and willingness to take personal and fiscal risks. Jones took himself seriously, but those around him could often see his foibles; and they would, with good humor, take note of his limitations and eccentricities. Commenting upon the passion he brought to his legislative responsibilities, the *Garden City Irrigator* observed on March 19, 1885 that the "Hon. C.J. Jones made his first appearance as a skater on Saturday evening, and did remarkably well for an amateur, although forced several times to sit down – something he was unaccustomed to while serving as legislator." Nevertheless, there is no question that Buffalo Jones was one of the best known citizens of Kansas in the early decades of the twentieth century.

The origins of where and when Jones obtained the name "Buffalo" are as obscure as to when, why, and with what justification he began to add the title "Colonel" to his name. Jones has no record of military service which would justify this rank. Inman maintains "colonel" was added to his name out of courtesy. Although the sources are some what unclear on this subject, some evidence suggests that Jones participated in the Pocket Canyon fight, or the battle of Yellow House Draw, on March 18, 1877. Distressed by the loss of freedom and the inadequate provisions provided for his people, Black Horse, a Comanche war chief, led a band of his followers from the Ft. Sill Reservation in mid December, 1876 to hunt buffalo in the Panhandle of West Texas and to attack any white buffalo hunters found there. In the battle which ensued between the Comanches and the buffalo hunters, Jones conducted himself with distinction. To recognize his prominence in this battle and to distinguish him from other plains buffalo hunters who bore the surname Jones, he began to be identified as "Buffalo Jones."[5]

1

Early Youth and Career of Charles Jesse Jones

His life began no more inauspiciously than that of many other Americans in the first half of the nineteenth century. He was born in a frontier cabin on January 31, 1844 in McLean County, Illinois, the second son in a family of twelve children. Responsibilities came quickly on the frontier, and childhood was fleeting amidst the many tasks that were necessary for survival. One of Jones' earliest companions was Elbert Hubbard, the founder of the Roycrofters. Hubbard later proclaimed that the county of their birth and youth was "a breeding-ground for wise men and virtuous."[6] It was not only the land of Lincoln but also the home of the Republican party which was founded in Bloomington, Illinois in 1856. His father, Noah Jones, was a frontier farmer who worked from sun to sun to provide for his family and build a future that justified such back breaking labor. With twelve children, his mother's labors were never finished. Strong anti-slavery passions were held by his father, and when these passions led to conflict with a local bully, Abraham Lincoln was retained for a $10 fee to defend his father's actions. While the story may be apocryphal, Jones developed from his earliest years an interest in frontier politics and would eagerly participate in local and state political activities.

Much of his early life was spent out of doors doing those chores that contributed to the family's successful existence. Wood was to be cut, weeds were to be chopped, animals were to be fed and watered, fields were to be plowed, stumps and rocks were to be removed. Nourished by these outdoor experiences, he developed a fondness for the wildlife of central Illinois. Although his family was often dependent upon venison and other game for sustenance, young Charles delighted in capturing young squirrels, birds, and rabbits for pets. Labor on his father's farms limited his education, and his life seemed destined to be days of unending physical labor.

As the Civil War drew to an end in 1865, he sought that education which had been denied him. He enrolled at Wesleyan University in Bloomington, Illinois. This institution had been established in 1850 by Methodist and civic leaders in Bloomington. By 1865, the one armed Civil War hero, and later explorer of the Colorado River and Grand Canyon, John Wesley Powell had joined the faculty as a professor of geology and natural history. Although he does not mention having classes with Professor Powell, Powell's interests and love of the outdoors would have paralleled those of Jones. In the tradition of Thoreau, Powell initiated the practice of teaching science by taking his students on field trips to examine flora and fauna in their natural settings. Although life as a student was less physically demanding than that of working in his father's fields, he became ill with typhoid fever. With his health and vision impaired, study became difficult. His formal education came to an end. Nevertheless, throughout his life Jones had a respect for education and demonstrated in his writing and lectures substantial awareness of developments in science, literature, and natural history.

In a world of imperfect medical knowledge, cures were often sought by seeking respite in new lands. The urge to follow the sun beyond the Mississippi River was strong in the Midwest, and Jones was captured by this impulse.   Restless by nature, he fulfilled that prophecy of an early western pioneer, "When God made man, He seemed to think it best, To make him in the East and let him travel West." Elbert Hubbard observed that "He is the pure type of the Middle West man who goes West and grows up with the country."[7]

By the spring of 1866, Jones had traveled west in a white hooded prairie schooner, a "mover-wagon," to Doniphan County in eastern Kansas.   His worldly possessions were a shirt, underwear, two pair of socks, a Bible, and Osage Orange (*Maclura pomifera*) seeds. Blond haired, blue eyed, six feet tall, and weighing one hundred and seventy pounds, the twenty-two year old Jones was determined to find his future in the five year old state of Kansas.

FORMER HOME (1866-1871) OF CHARLES J. AND MARTHA JONES IN TROY, DONIPHAN COUNTY, KANSAS. THIS PHOTO CIRCA 1990.

Settling in Troy, Kansas, he established a nursery with George D. Baker and sought to supply Osage Orange trees to other settlers. While it could be used as lumber and fuel, its principal use was either as fence posts or as an almost impenetrable hedge. When planted in rows in close proximity to one another, it formed a barrier through which cattle, hogs, and sheep could not pass. Osage Orange solved one of the persistent problems of the prairie – the construction of a fence which prevented one's livestock from wandering. This relative of the mulberry, with its hard wood, long thorns, and enduring quality as hedge or fence posts, was a practical solution to a western dilemma. It was an inexpensive, but labor intensive, solution to the persistent frontier problem of fencing. In later years, Jones sought to settle another problem of western settlement, the delivery of water to arid lands.

From 1866 to 1871, Jones labored to develop his nursery for Osage Orange and fruit trees, promising the new state's settlers that he could supply Kansas grown apple, peach, cherry, quince, and pear trees as well as flowers, shrubbery, and grapes. In 1867, most of his nursery was lost to a plague of Rocky Mountain Locusts. Never daunted by adversity, he was always confident that through hard work he would be successful. In the winter and spring of 1867 and 1868, he grafted almost 50,000 fruit trees and acquired numerous grape vines for his nursery. Appearing in enormous swarms, the locusts returned again in the summer of 1868 eating everything but the mortgage, some observers remarked. Jones once more had to begin again. This new beginning included a significant change in his personal life.

On January 20, 1869, Jones married Martha Walton, a descendant of the famous seventeenth century English naturalist, fisherman, and author Isaak Walton. Although now married, Jones still believed that his future lay over the next swale of prairie slightly beyond the reaches of civilization. The thought of pulling weeds, tending fruit trees, and pruning grape vines so that they could be consumed by periodic invasions of Rocky Mountain Locusts was not as inviting a future as moving further west to claim new lands.

CHARLES JESSE JONES (CIRCA 1869) AT APPROXIMATELY AGE 25.

MARTHA J. WALTON (CIRCA 1869), POSSIBLY AT THE TIME OF HER ENGAGEMENT TO JONES.

2

Jones Finds His Future
Upon the Plains

On New Year's day 1872, in the midst of a frigid Kansas winter, Jones found himself two hundred miles from his wife and stone home at Troy. Here on the southern fork of the Solomon River in Osborne County, the Homestead Act of 1862 allowed him to claim 160 acres of verdant prairie soil. In April of 1872, accompanied by his wife and new son, he set forth for his new homestead. Troy, and his experiences as a nurseryman, were in his past. In his journal, he describes life as a Kansas homesteader. "In the summer of 1872, I was an embryo farmer on the new prairies of western Kansas, which region just then began to attract immigrants on account of its superiority of soil and climate."[8] To augment their income, he hunted and captured buffalo; and in later years, he stated "that was the year I determined to 'some sweet day' capture a herd, domesticate and perpetuate the species."[9] If we presume that his later memory is substantially correct, and only modestly enhanced by image building, then this becomes the year in which Jones' career as a preserver of the American bison begins. In that year he captured about a dozen buffalo and sold them for seven and a half dollars each. These would be the first recorded buffalo captured by Jones, the individual who in the history of the American West captured more buffalo than any other individual.

When Jones arrived in Kansas, there were more buffalo in the great southern herd than there were people in the United States. Yet, by 1872 the numbers of this great host had been halved by hide and meat hunters.

The stage was set for the replacement of the red man's buffalo by the white man's buffalo – the Texas Longhorn. For Jones, as for many prairie settlers, buffalo provided a source of income and food that allowed them to maintain themselves in a demanding and economically limited environment. Hunting buffalo was a lucrative frontier activity, for a hunter and skinner could make anywhere from $25 to $50 a day. Yet, this was an industry in western Kansas that only began to emerge after the end of the Civil War. It was then that eastern and European tanneries discovered that thick buffalo hides could be tanned for harness leather and made into drive belts for an increasingly industrialized America. As railroads became arteries of transportation in the heart of America, they provided the means for shipping the large and unwieldy dried hides back east. Still later, they carried tons of bones, horns and elk and deer antlers back east for the sugar, button, and china industries. After the Civil War, larger caliber and more effective rifles became available to hunt the buffalo. With his Sharps .44 sporting rifle, Jones became a skilled prairie hunter.

Sharps 45 Rifle of
Charles Jesse "Buffalo" Jones
Preserver of the Buffalo

AN 1878 SHARPS .45 CALIBER RIFLE OWNED BY C.J. "BUFFALO"JONES.

As his proficiency evolved, Jones often killed ten of these great animals a day. Farming was not as exhilarating as hunting the shaggy monarch of the plains. Jones began to devote more attention to the pursuit of the bison than to following in the furrows of his plow. From 1874 to 1878, Jones dedicated more and more time and energy to hunting the buffalo while living at Sterling, in Rice County, Kansas. There, in the Arkansas River Valley, Jones increased his knowledge of the habits and life history of the buffalo. This awareness of the natural history of the bison became invaluable when he began to capture buffalo calves in order to preserve the declining herds. For the balance of his life, Jones is praised frequently for his skills as a hunter and for his knowledge of the wildlife which he is pursuing.

A YOUNG C.J. JONES CAPTURING BUFFALO CALVES.

Ever restless and curious about what lay over the horizon, Jones wandered farther west seeking buffalo, antelope, and wild horses along the Arkansas River. Thus, he entered that arid region with which he would be identified for the balance of his life. By 1879, he had moved to those lands along the banks of the Arkansas River that became the future site of Garden City, Kansas. Jones became one of the most ardent promoters of this emerging community and a significant factor in its growth. Other founders of Garden City were William and James Fulton. Born in Pennsylvania, these brothers had lived in Rice County, Kansas supporting themselves by capturing wild horse, and hunting buffalo and antelope. It was their dream to have a more sedentary life, and in March 1878, they filed adjacent homesteads in the unorganized Sequoyah

County west of Dodge City. By filing in what they thought was almost the exact center of the county adjacent to the Arkansas River, they believed that they had selected a site that would inevitably become the county seat. As a county seat, their proposed community would have a powerful impetus for success. Success would be even more likely if they could complement its geographical and proposed political advantage with access to a railroad line.

With the aid of Charles Van Trump, the Dodge City surveyor for Ford County, they determined the precise location of their homesteads and filed their claims on March 16, 1878 at the land office in Larned, Kansas. William Fulton filed on the southeast quarter section 18-24-32, his brother James filed on the southwest quarter of the same section. The remaining two quarters (160 acres each) of this section were to be filed on by Van Trump and John A. Stevens.

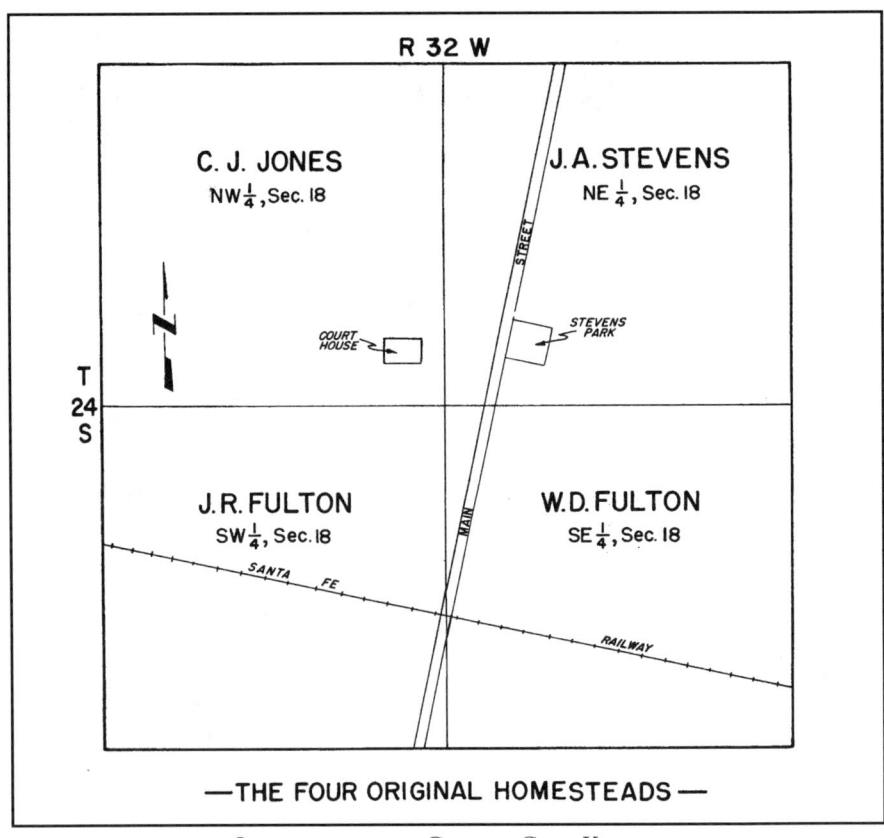

ORIGINAL PLAT OF GARDEN CITY, KANSAS.

Unfortunately, their carefully laid plans were complicated by a filing error in the land office. Both Van Trump and Stevens were shown to have filed on the same northeastern quarter. Stevens built a cabin on this quarter and began to prove up his homestead claim when another settler, discovering that the northwest quarter was vacant, filed a timber claim upon it. Van Trump was left without a claim. Jones, along with other members of the Sterling community, saw promise in this undeveloped region. Jones persuaded the timber claimant to relinquish his claim for $90 and a gold watch.[10] Confusion over land claims and title were not unique to this area, and accounts such as this could be repeated for almost every county in the state and every state beyond the Mississippi River. The Garden City town site was now composed of two quarter sections (160 acres each) in the southeast and southwest held by the Fulton brothers and the northwest quarter section (later known as the Jones Addition) held by Jones and northeast quarter section (later known as the Stevens addition) held by J.A. Stevens. Jones and Stevens soon became major competitors with each other over the development of their particular holdings.

GARDEN CITY, KANSAS HOMESTEAD (CIRCA 1938)
OF CHARLES J. AND MARTHA JONES.

3

Buffalo Jones and the Rise of Garden City

So enters Buffalo Jones upon the stage of Garden City history. Only a boomer, speculator, or dreamer would have seen promise and future for this wind swept, arid, treeless land in the Arkansas River Valley. While the Atchison, Topeka and Santa Fe's rail line passed through the proposed new community on its way to Colorado, there were no plans for trains to stop there. To the south of the proposed new community were the Sand Hills; although often alive with game, they contained little that would welcome settlement. Herds of buffalo, bands of wild horses, and numbers of fleet footed antelope could often be seen from the new town site itself.

It was in this seemingly environmentally disadvantaged community that Jones was enlisted by the Fulton brothers to attract other settlers. He approached this task with the same enthusiasm that he pursued a herd of buffalo. He linked his future to the success of this community. Jones persuaded prospective settlers traveling west in Kansas to inspect the possibilities in this new community. Realizing that without a commitment from the Santa Fe to stop at Garden City growth would be limited, Jones was dispatched to Topeka to persuade the railroad to establish a station there. Persuasive and optimistic about the community's opportunities, and authorized to grant the Santa Fe 160 acres in the new town site, Jones received a commitment to build a depot on non-railroad land. While it was rare for a railroad to agree to such an arrangement, it was a major coup for Garden City. For now prospective settlers could be delivered to the community to inspect the lands there, mail could be delivered, and commodities and goods could be delivered and shipped. The Santa Fe shipped in an 80-foot-long prefabricated depot and the carpenters to assemble it. By early May of 1879, the community of some 250, with a thousand more in the county, had its depot and a future. For a brief period, Jones served as station agent until he resigned on June 19, 1879. Garden City was now linked to the world beyond southwest Kansas.

By the spring of 1879, Jones was actively engaged in the "selling" of Garden City to prospective settlers, and his energy was acknowledged by the small but growing community. *The Garden City Paper* which began publication on April 3, 1879 frequently recognized his role in the community's growth. Indeed, until the paper ceased publication on October 30, 1879, no other community figure was mentioned as frequently in its columns. His hunting exploits, role in showing and selling land, producing agricultural crops, acts of civic responsibility, and efforts to promote the community were reported almost weekly. The Editor of the *Ellinwood Express* observed that "C.J. Jones seems to be the leading spirit of the community, and is doing much toward settling up the country."[11] Jones provided free horses and buggies daily to show prospective buyers and homesteaders land and property and would aid them in preparing their homestead papers, and filing their final proofs. He was an agent as well for the Garden City Town Co. and even developed a method for sending bank drafts by wire.

To aid in the sale and settlement of land, he developed a relationship with the land office in Larned, Kansas that allowed him to learn which lands had already been claimed and when new immigrants arrived in western Kansas seeking land. Through daily telegraph messages, he was apprised of the most recent claims, developments, and new arrivals. With a growing awareness of the usefulness of a knowledge of law in his expanding endeavors, he began to more systematically order his legal experiences. Ultimately, Jones was admitted to the Kansas bar, and this legal recognition helped him in his many sales and land transactions.[12] To aid settlers who were cash poor, Jones advised them of the potential of the land, and how they might feed their families with the buffalo, deer, and antelope that could be found in the Sand Hills south of town, and how, if necessary, they could collect and sell buffalo bones for $6 a ton. Buffalo bones were a significant commodity in western Kansas, and bone collectors were found frequently on the prairies. Indeed, bones were legal tender in southwest Kansas.[13] The bones would be shipped back east and converted to fertilizer, carbonized and used to process brown sugar into finer grained white sugar, and ground up and used to make light and translucent bone china. The more adventuresome could capture wild horses from the herds that were often found in the vicinity of the city. If one questioned Jones' veracity about the abundance of wildlife that could be found in the immediate region to provide for one's family, Jones could call upon his hunting experiences in the region and share with them his successes. On December 11, 1884, Jones and three companions returned from a ten day hunt where they reported that they had taken 18 deer, 28 antelope, 6 wolves, and many small game.[14]

There is hardly any community endeavor in which Jones was not involved - from the buying, selling, and construction of office space, to the supervision of a bridge over the Arkansas,[15] to becoming director of a second street car company in Garden City,[16] or assuming a position as a director of a community newspaper.[17]

When it was noted that Garden City was a sun-baked, treeless comunity, Jones imported a train car load of cottonwood saplings from Sterling to be planted along Main Street. It was observed that "if the desert does not bloom like the rose, it will not be the fault of C.J. Jones."[18] Unfortunately, in a land of little rain, trees require both moisture and attention. Few young cottonwoods survived the dry conditions of 1879. In 1883, Jones planted and watered trees along Main Street and the three streets adjacent to it. For those which were alive in the fall, he was going to receive 10 cents a tree.[19] Jones' persistent rival, J.A. Stevens announced less than a week later that he was going to plant 5,000 dwarf fruit trees to beautify the surroundings.[20] The public did not respond as completely as Jones wished for the 10 cents payment per tree on their property; on December 20, 1883, Jones warned the community that the city council had given him permission to dig up all the trees that he had planted if they were not paid for within the next thirty days.[21] It was the prediction of *The Garden City Irrigator* that the "Time will come when Garden City will be a veritable Oasis in the heart of the Great American Desert."[22] While it was anticipated that Jones' trees would contribute to the emergence of this oasis, like most of his ventures there was more promise than fulfillment.

Among the most prominent of the early citizens attracted to Garden City by Jones was Frederick Finnup. While Finnup was not a founder of Garden City, he certainly was one of its earliest builders. He purchased the first lot from the Garden City Town Company and began a long and beneficial relationship with this community. Blessed with both access to capital and confidence in himself and his new home, Finnup supported those individuals who could contribute to building a strong foundation for the city. He strengthened the community in many diverse ways as a builder, city father, and merchant.

Jones' talents as a dedicated "booster" of Garden City are revealed in an article prepared by a Special Correspondent of *The Kansas City Journal* in June of 1879:

> "In the upper Arkansas Valley, 418 miles by rail from Kansas City, and 70 miles from the West line of the State. 'What is it?
> 'It is the best three months' town in Kansas, with forty good buildings, fifteen of which are two stories high, and one of which has a larger hall than can be found west of Hutchinson. It is the only point of consequence between Dodge City and Las Animas, and it is the prospective capital of Sequoyah County, and the seat of a new U.S. Land District. We have the finest body of government land now vacant in the valley, and can offer greater inducements to emigrants than any other area in Kansas. Come up, and we will make those statements good and throw in an antelope and wild horse hunt for good measure.'
>
> This conversation occurred between your correspondent and Hon. C.J. 'Buffalo' Jones of Garden City on the west bound Santa Fe train, which in due time landed us in this brisk little village of the 'sun bright wilderness.' I am agreeably disappointed at the appearance of the town and country, and am inclined to believe my enthusiastic friend will realize his high hopes."[23] (*The Garden City Paper*, July 3, 1879)

This is an interesting passage for not only does it speak to Jones' talents as a booster of Garden City, but it also is one of the earliest, if not the earliest, references to him as "Buffalo" Jones. Deemed "irrepressible" by the local paper, he was described with some accuracy as an individual who was "always at the front and full of business."[24] On the fourth of July, 1879, Jones was selected to read the Declaration of Independence at the community celebration of the nation's birthday. Later in the day, he came second in a shooting match after hitting ten of fifteen eggs that were thrown into the air as targets.[25] His talents as a skilled marksman were not all hyperbole.

If Jones' business was to successfully promote Garden City, then indeed it had to be shown that gardens and crops would grow in profusion in this arid land – a region which was described so often in print as the "Great American Desert." Frequently, throughout 1879, Jones visited the local newspaper office with agricultural products that exceeded expectations. On July 3, 1879, he produced a stalk of corn that was six feet high and five inches in circumference;[26] on July 17th, he presented the editors with some millet which they described, not unsurprisingly, "as fine a specimen of the kind we ever saw,"[27] and on July 31st he brought to their office a piece of spear grass from the river bottom that was sixty eight feet long.[28]

Entrance to fairgrounds at foot of the hill on North Fourth Street, Garden City, Kansas (1886). Jones with some of his buffalo in the background.

He later presented the editors with a stalk of millet that measured "four feet and three inches high."[29] Although Jones's principal activity was the sale and promotion of land in the county, he also engaged in farming and became the first to plant wheat with a drill in Sequoyah County. Jones was also a plaintiff in the first law suit filed in Garden City.[30]

The newspaper's interest in agricultural activities should be anticipated in a rural paper seeking to promote the settlement of the community. In the cash poor economy of the region where buffalo bones were accepted in lieu of cash, *The Garden City Paper* would "take any kind of produce on subscription from peanuts to pumpkins." [31]

It was in the railroad's interest for the community to prosper, and so they acceded to Jones' lobbying to have seeds shipped to Garden City for the same rates that they were shipped to Dodge City, fifty-four miles to the east. Indeed, thinking of the future, the Santa Fe went a step further and agreed to provide seed wheat to settlers in two-bushel sacks with the company bearing "all the expense of buying, hauling, transporting, and shrinkage. The settlers pay only the actual cost of the wheat and for sacks. Care will be taken to buy only varieties that have proved successful in our state, and that is free from smut, cheat, and rye as possible." [32]

The specter of drought was another impediment to settlement that Jones and other promoters of the community had to confront. The newspaper aided their efforts by seeking to dispel such perceptions. In an August, 1879, editorial they observed somewhat enthusiastically that

> "When men who have never seen this country, nor ever
> heard anything from a reliable source about it, say we have no
> rain out here, and that it is no more of a farming country than
> the Desert of the Sahara, know about as much about it as a
> hog does about holidays. The saying that nothing can be raised
> west of the 100th Meridian is all humbug, as our crops now
> growing will amply prove. You can't tell that class of men
> anything about this country. They know all about it, and still
> they have never seen it, and couldn't tell whether people out
> here subsist on grasshoppers or tarantulas.[33]"

Regardless of the paper's protestations, the lack of rainfall sufficient for dry land farming was a problem, and the periodic droughts discouraged settlement and encouraged settlers to leave their land perhaps reciting that oft heard Kansas phrase, "in God we trusted, in Kansas we busted." Southwestern Kansas was blessed with higher than normal precipitation from 1878 to 1886 and crops grew copiously; but climate is a fickle friend, and that which has been may not be in the future. When the traditional patterns of drought began to return in 1887 and rainfall fell to its more normal averages, crop production and optimism about agriculture in this region declined precipitously. The solution to this dilemma was irrigation, and Jones played an active role in seeking to bring water to this land.

Many realized that agriculture in the Arkansas River Valley would always be limited if farmers were dependent only upon rain fall. The unpredictability of an annual water supply for farmers' crops encouraged sundry attempts to find more of this precious resource. While the vain dreams of the rain makers, or pluviculturalists, might be tried in other areas of western Kansas, in southwestern Kansas, the drought of 1879 encouraged the development of ditch irrigation which would divert waters from the Arkansas River.

EARLY DITCH IRRIGATION IN FINNEY COUNTY, KANSAS.

By September of 1882, there were thirty-three miles of irrigation ditches in the county. Although Jones would not be involved in the first attempt at irrigation in this area, he would be intimately involved in many of the later attempts. The first substantial irrigation system built in southwestern Kansas, The Garden City Ditch, was planned and constructed by W. H. Armentrout[34] in late 1879. When it was reported that using this irrigation system, Squire Worrell produced in 1881, 400 bushels of Irish potatoes per acre, 600 bushels of sweet potatoes an acre, 4,000 head of cabbage per acre, 8,000 melons per acre, 1,000 turnips per acre, and 20 – 25 bushels of wheat per acre, other settlers wanted access to such waters. With such productivity in an arid land, it was not surprising that Worrell's farm was selected as the nation's model farm in 1882.[35] The community's success with irrigation encouraged European and eastern settlers and speculators to visit Garden City.

Jones clearly wished to explore the opportunities presented in irrigated land. In Kearny County alone, Jones chartered four irrigation ditches. Beginning in 1880, he helped to survey, develop, and construct the Kansas Ditch which drew water out of the Arkansas River west of Garden City near Sherlock (Holcomb). By July, 1881, farmers were receiving water from this ditch. Jones sold his interest in this system a year later.[36] An early student of this subject was critical of Jones' involvement in these endeavors, remarking that "C.J. Jones, always scheming and ready to promote anything he thought there was money in, took out a charter for what was known as the Minnehaha Ditch. In fact, Jones had a dozen charters for irrigation ditches along the Arkansas River. He surveyed the ditch himself, and did some work for about two miles. He received a little money from the southside people for what he had done. The ditch was taken out on the south bank of the Arkansas in 1880, about two miles west of Lakin. It was abandoned without ever being used."[37]

Almost always persuasive when promoting southwestern Kansas, Jones continued his support of irrigation schemes. In 1881, he found support from business and university interests in Lawrence for construction of a ditch that would provide irrigation waters for lands west of Lakin, south and east of Deerfield, north of Sherlock for ten miles, and all lands north of the Kansas Ditch. The ditch and laterals were to be surveyed by F.O. Marvin, a professor of engineering at the University of Kansas.[38] Work on the Great Eastern Canal began in October, 1881; and by the summer of 1882, much of the work on the canal was complete although water was not sold to farmers until 1884. While Jones excelled at promotion, he seldom profited to the degree he expected, or wished, from his project. His returns on the Great Eastern Canal were modest. Farmers around Deerfield were the most advantaged by this system.

Seldom daunted by the turn of events, Jones lent his talents to the promotion of the Amazon Ditch, another irrigation system deriving waters from the Arkansas River. Projected as the largest irrigation system in the region, it was to have its head gates five miles west of Hartland on the north side of the Arkansas River. After drawing water from the river, its ditches and laterals were to irrigate lands not yet provided with water. Its main canal would have flowed for more than ninety-nine and a half miles through Kearny, Finney, the southern reaches of Scott, and along the west side of Gray counties. It would have had 75 miles of main laterals and 100 miles of farm and sub-laterals.[39] The project was plagued by litigation, design difficulties, construction delays, and financial problems. Demands upon the Arkansas River in Colorado and Kansas were beginning to limit the water available for irrigation, and the massive Amazon Ditch was never completed. Jones conveyed his interests in this project to the Southwest Kansas Land and Irrigation Company in August, 1889.[40] The enduring conflict between Kansas and Colorado over water rights in the Arkansas River had its beginning in these nineteenth century developments. Enduringly persistent about the future of Southwest Kansas, Jones joined other members of the growing community in attempting to engage the governor of Kansas in this area of the state.

The social highlight of Garden City's first year was a hunt arranged by Jones for the Governor of Kansas, John Pierce St. John, and the Mayor of Topeka. When the eighth governor of Kansas visited Garden City on this hunt, it brought visible recognition to an emerging community. It was a coup for Jones to arrange such a visit. Arriving on October 8, 1879, they quickly departed for Lakin, and then moved eight miles to the northwest to hunt buffalo, antelope, and other prairie animals. After a successful hunt of ten days, they returned to Garden City as the guest of Jones to celebrate their success in the field. The whole community turned out to welcome the party, but Governor St. John did not remain long at Garden City. He had many pressing issues to attend to: the 1879 Kansas legislature was addressing the significant questions of auditing the 1878 Indian claims, the appointment of John Ingalls to the U.S. Senate, the calling of a new constitutional convention, and a prohibition amendment.

Garden City continued to grow and on January 13, 1883, it became an incorporated city of the third class with approximately 300 citizens. On January 26, 1883 after an election in which thirty-four votes were cast, C.J. Jones was elected the city's first mayor. The early ordinances of the newly incorporated city addressed the pressing problems of the community. Cattle and livestock were not permitted to run loose in the city; trains could not block thoroughfares for more than five minutes; and property owners were expected to erect hitching posts in front of their premises to prevent thoughtless individuals from hitching their horses to the limited trees in the community.[41] The prospects for future growth were enhanced when, on October 1, 1883, the United States Land Office for the Southwestern Land District opened in Garden City.[42]

LAND OFFICE IN GARDEN CITY, KANSAS (CIRCA 1883)

People came to the city to file their claims, to litigate their claims, and to speculate on their claims and properties. The office did a "land office" business until 1889 when the depression hit western Kansas. The office was closed in January, 1894.[43] To encourage individuals to settle in this region, Garden City and Finney County needed to continually publicize their advantages. On May 17, 1883, Jones hosted 96 editors of the Kansas Editorial Association on a tour of the farms, ranches, irrigating ditches, and commercial and residential properties of the county. To make it a more memorable occasion, the editors experienced as well a jack rabbit chase with some of the greyhounds which Jones always kept. The day concluded with an antelope dinner.[44]

On October 1, 1884, Finney County was officially organized out of the unorganized counties of Sequoyah and Arapaho (presently, Haskell County) and portions of Kearny, Grant, Lane, Gray, and Meade counties. Named after Lieutenant Governor Finney, with its 2880 square miles, it became for a time the largest county in Kansas. On November 4, 1884, Jones was elected a representative to the state legislature, serving as a representative not only in 1884 but also in 1885 and 1888.

JONES AS A KANSAS STATE LEGISLATOR (CIRCA 1884)

Jones enjoyed politics. Politics gave him access to powerful men and institutions which might advance his interests as well as the communities he was seeking to advance. In June 1884, he was an alternate member of the Kansas Delegation to the National Republican Convention in Chicago. Here, Jones played a role in the nomination of James G. Blaine, the "Plumed Knight." That belied his humble status as an alternate delegate from the state of Kansas. At a crucial moment in the nominating process, Jones entered the Convention Hall carrying a large banner with a black rooster on the top of it. The rooster had around his neck a card which said "Kansas Crows!! For Her Loyal Delegates, Kansas 50,000 for the nominee, 75,000 for James G. Blaine." The sight of this banner and the accompanying band playing patriotic music crystallized support for the Plumed Knight and John A. Logan; and their nominations carried.

Jones, always willing to profit from an opportunity, reproduced color lithographs of the banner with him carrying it to sell to loyal Kansas Republicans.[46] Jones thought that no Kansas home could resist having this 40 1/4" x 29 1/4" print on their walls. Unfortunately in the bitter presidential campaign of 1884, questions of Blaine's integrity and the defection of the 'mugwump' Republicans led to the election of the Democratic candidate, Grover Cleveland. There were few sales of the lithograph.

Garden City, enjoying and prospering in the boom years of 1885 – 1887, could not anticipate the bust that would occur in the last years of the 1880s. Thousands made their way to western Kansas. As a land speculator, Jones and his rival John A. Stevens had many opportunities to prosper, but each was fearful that the other had more prospects. By 1886, the city's population reached six thousand, and speculators and real estate agents had created approximately fifty large and small additions with lots for sale in each of them.

Although property values were inflated, there seemed to be no end to the boom. Jones and Stevens, with the largest additions, made substantial investments in buildings and other developments. Stevens built the Opera House and the four-story, brick Windsor Hotel, while Jones constructed the famous "Buffalo Block" and planned a ten mile Jones Avenue through his addition. The "Buffalo Block," also known as the Jones' Marble Block, was built of native, white, limestone quarried at Kendall, Kansas. It consisted of a large, three story building much of which was devoted to the "Buffalo Hotel."

JONES MARBLE BLOCK IN GARDEN CITY, KANSAS (CIRCA 1885-86)

The hotel contained 80 guest rooms, decorated in a Queen Anne style, with a handsome interior staircase and elaborate inner court covered by a glass roof. The cost of the building and furnishings was calculated to be $50,000.[57] As the

Finney County Directory contended, such structures as those built by Jones and Stevens were appropriate for this community since "No where in the state can be found a better class of people than the inhabitants of Garden City; her business men are noted for their enterprise, for seeing sagacity and general intelligence. They leave nothing undone which will advance the material prosperity of the town and county. Every commendable enterprise receives their hearty and generous support."[48]

Jones and Stevens assumed continued growth and prosperity for the community and region; and when this failed to materialize, they were financially over extended and had to liquidate their assets for pennies on the dollar. A dedicated early student of the development of Finney County and southwest Kansas provides a perceptive assessment of the early developers of Garden City: "The three leading builders of the city had been C.J. Jones, John A. Stevens, and Frederick Finnup. Jones had lost everything and had gone elsewhere to engage in other enterprises, as he was never idle. Stevens had lost practically everything, and was blocking up a little ranch by getting tax-deeds to several sections of land in north Haskell County. Frederick Finnup was still holding his property, but it had depreciated in value for years and was not saleable."[49]

Jones was a settler, developer, and speculator like many of his peers in Garden City. His uniqueness lies in the many diverse areas in which he was willing to speculate. Indeed, it is difficult to find any area of the frontier economy in which he did not engage in some economic wishful thinking. Learning of the successful flight of the Wright brothers in December 1903, Jones let it be known that he also was in the act of creating an airplane. While serving as Game Warden in Yellowstone National Park, Jones sold one of the scouts whom he supervised a $100 interest in a balloon-propelling device which he claimed he was going to exhibit at the St. Louis World Fair.[50] Before Jones is criticized too excessively for such grandiose dreams, let it be known that you can not find a state in the union where at least one individual did not claim to be doing, or thinking of doing, the same thing the Wrights were doing.

The future of Garden City and southwestern Kansas was linked not only to the availability of irrigated land but also to reasonable shipping rates. With only one railroad line serving Garden City and the southwest, the Santa Fe could establish what ever rates it wished. Among the most heated issues confronting farmers in the last decades of the nineteenth century was the lack of regulation of railroad shipping rates. Railroads in many areas of the west had a virtual monopoly over service, shipping, and transportation costs. To encourage the building of railroads and settlement of the west, railroad companies received twenty square miles of land for every mile of track that they laid. In addition, they were expected to haul government freight, materials, personnel, and supplies at a reduced rate. In 1946, when this federal rate reduction was abandoned, it was estimated that the railroads had repaid the value of the lands granted to them ten times over.

Garden City leaders wanted additional railroad lines so that there would be rate and service competition. On May 26, Jones entertained R.R. Cable, President of the Rock Island Railroad Company, four members of his executive board, and other distinguished guests who were making a luxury tour of the Rocky Mountain west. They wished to view Jones's herd of buffalo, the largest herd of bison still alive. Jones provided carriages and buggies which took the party to his ranch. He then accompanied President Cable in his luxury railroad cars to the Colorado border. Jones used this occasion to lobby the Rock Island for service to Garden City. Cable spoke candidly observing that "he should be pleased to extend a branch of the Rock Island system to our city, but that he was not prepared to talk encouragingly at the present time. He said that the state could not expect much more railroad building until it had produced another crop, and what was true in regard to Kansas was true to the entire west; that a failure of crops and the multiplication of lines, together with unfavorable national and state legislation, had largely depreciated railroad securities and that capital was not seeking investment in them with the avidity that was noticeable a couple of years ago, and that it was difficult to float the bonds of extensions or new lines unless they penetrated a fertile and well developed territory."[51] Many wished to have additional train service to Garden City and Finney County and southwest Kansas. By May 31, 1887, twenty-seven charters were filed with the state to build a railroad to service these areas. By 1900, forty such charters had been filed.[52] Buffalo Jones would be involved in seven of these charters all of which passed through Garden City. To justify their existence, and to avoid the appearance of not competing directly with the Santa Fe, all seven of these proposed trains would have north – south routes. It was only the Garden City Nickel Plate Railway Company that went beyond speculative discussion. Some fifty miles of grade were prepared for this rail road from Garden City to Dighton, Kansas, but no rolling stock was acquired or any rails laid. By early 1890, Jones was focusing more upon the preservation of the buffalo.

4

Buffalo Jones and the Preservation of the American Bison

When his fortunes began to fail in Garden City and his numerous mortgages began to be called, Jones turned his attention to capitalizing upon the future of the buffalo. While Jones might claim that 1872 was the crucial date in his decision to preserve the buffalo, it was not until fourteen years later that he began to implement his plans to save the American bison.

"I had been a successful buffalo-hunter, had killed thousands for their hides, but the idea of my buffalo-rescuing project was but a creature of the brain, not yet perfectly formulated; yet that was the year I determined to 'some sweet day' capture a herd, domesticate and perpetuate the species. I captured about a dozen that year, sold them for seven dollars and a half each, and was delighted to receive even that much.[53]

The problem with this particular statement is that it is difficult to identify a period of time when Jones, up to this point in his career, could have been a hide hunter. Undoubtedly, he may have hunted them by this time, but those hunts must have been occasional and for meat or sport rather than for hides. Given the detail that Jones includes in the narration of other events in his life, it seems likely that if he had been a hide hunter he would have described these activities in greater details in the materials he gave to Inman. The above passage is the first reference to his having captured any buffalo. When the remoteness of his homestead, the difficulties he experienced in farming, and his desire to have more opportunities for his family led to their moving to Sterling, Kansas, he might have had the opportunity to become a hide hunter.[54] The devastating winter of 1885-1886 changed not only the life of Charles Jesse Jones but also modified dramatically the range cattle industry of the Great Plains.

The blizzards of 1885 - 1886 altered the nature of the range cattle industry, and for Jones became an experience that shaped his interest in domesticating the buffalo for the nation's use. Snow had fallen frequently in the last months of 1885, and in the first week of the New Year a blizzard swept through the Plains. Temperatures dropped to 30° below zero, prairie grasses were covered with crusted snow, and drifts more than six feet high were common. In a futile measure of self preservation cattle turned their tails to the wind and drifted down wind seeking shelter. Relief was not to be found, and exposure to constant wind, snow, and low temperatures led to the death of thousands of cattle. Losses for some ranches and Kansas cattle companies reached more than seventy percent. The range cattle industry with its characteristic long horns would never recover from this winter storm. Approximately 100 Kansans lost their lives as a result of these blizzards. The Kansas State Board of Agriculture reported that cattle had died along the railroad tracks leading to that city in such numbers that trains could not proceed until the carcasses were removed. Cattle were found stacked five deep along the Arkansas River. Jones' interest in preserving the buffalo was never for nostalgic, aesthetic, historic or wilderness concerns. He had no interest in this animal in its relationship to Indian society. He was quite utilitarian when developing reasons for why this animal should be preserved. In public lecture after public lecture given in later years, Jones observed that in March of 1886 while traveling from Kansas to Texas, he saw "thousands of the carcasses of domestic cattle which had 'drifted' before the chilling, freezing, 'norther.' Every one of them had died with its tail to the blizzard, never having stopped except at its last breath, then fell dead in its tracks. When I reached the habitat of the buffalo, not one of their carcasses was visible, except those which had been slain by hunters."[55] Caught in a spring storm himself, he thought about what he had seen.

Thinking about the differences between the "white man's domestic cattle and the red man's cattle (buffalo)," Jones notes that he thought "Why not chain this great giant? . . . Why not domesticate this wonderful beast which can endure such a 'blizzard,' defying a storm so destructive to our domestic species? Why not infuse this hardy blood into our native cattle, and have a perfect animal, one that will defy all these elements?"[56]

C.J. Jones training two harnessed and yoked buffalo,
an experiment in breaking buffalo to work

In a lengthy soliloquy on this animal, he made these points:

> The buffalo is king of the blizzard; he was constructed for
> the fitful climate of the Great Plains; he was made for the use
> of a race that had nothing else to depend upon, and must
> surely be nearly a perfect creation. His flesh is far superior to
> that of any domestic animal under similar conditions; his robe
> is 'solid comfort' when the wintry blasts howl. The hair of the
> animal's head and forehead is heavy and springy, serving
> perfectly the office of a mattress and pillow. Its tallow is as rich
> and palatable as butter; the flesh, when dried serves for bread;
> the hide, when tanned, makes good shoes, rope, and leather.
> Its fur is softer than lamb's wool, and when woven into cloth is
> the lightest and warmest fabric ever manufactured. The under
> fur is like swan's down, and makes a perfectly waterproof hat
> when converted into that article. The rain is shed from it as
> rapidly as from a duck's back; it is this wise provision of nature
> so close to their bodies which keeps the animal constantly dry
> and warm. While domestic cattle are stricken down by the
> deadly venom of the rattlesnake, the buffalo receive its fangs in

the long hair and wool covering their head and legs, and then trample the serpents into the earth with their sharp hoofs. Its fleece may be carded off every spring, after having fulfilled its purpose of a winter's protection to the animal, woven into the finest fabrics, knitted into hosiery, and made into robes and blankets which kings and princes delight to recline under.

The buffalo's endurance is marvelous; as a beast of burden it has no superior. The milk of the buffalo cow is infinitely richer than that of the Jersey. The buffalo are decidedly clannish; they do not stray away , neither can they be driven off their range by the severest 'blizzard,' and in contradistinction to the domestic steer, always face the storm.

Their sense of smell is so keen, they can tell where a rich bunch of grass is, though buried a foot deep under the snow. They root in snow like a razor-back hog after artichokes. The severest winter has no pangs for these patient brutes. Their sinews serve as thread for heavy sewing; their horns make excellent goblets, receptacles for powder and beautiful buttons. Their fur spun into yarn affords the best material for hosiery and underwear. Their bones can be converted into handles for ladles and cutlery. When ground, they furnish the best fertilizer for an impoverished soil; when charred, are used by sugar-works in the process of refining.

Where, then is the animal to be found which can compare with the buffalo, the rejected buffalo? . . . So it is with the buffalo: when we have fitted it to its proper sphere, it is the chief of all ruminants.[57]

After this enthusiastic, remarkable, and not always accurate, delineation of the desirable characteristics of this "chief of all ruminants," Jones outlines his plan for this animal. "I will chain him, and domesticate a race of cattle equal to, if not superior to all ruminants heretofore known."[58] To demonstrate its utility, he further notes that he is going to dress himself "entirely in clothing made from the products of the buffalo; even the buttons of my clothes shall be made of horns and hoofs of that wonderful animal." Although he failed to dress himself entirely in clothing made from buffalo products, he did begin to wear a full length buffalo coat whenever weather permitted.

COLONEL JONES DRESSED IN GARMENTS PRODUCED FROM FUR OF BUFFALO AND CATALO.

COLONEL JONES IN BUFFALO HIDE COAT.

Near the end of April, 1886, Jones and two companions set forth from Kendall, on the Arkansas River in southwestern Kansas, for the Panhandle of Texas to capture buffalo calves. After passing across the *Llano Estacado*, and with adventures that might be expected in such a quest, fourteen calves were captured, nursed on condensed milk, and brought safely back to Jones' ranch at Garden City, Kansas. This was the stock with which he was going to "perpetuate the species."[60] While returning from Texas, near the Canadian River, Jones proclaimed that he saw not one but three white buffalo grazing in a mixed herd of buffalo and cattle.[61] In later years, Jones claimed that instead of white buffalo, he had seen "nothing more or less than exact prototypes of 'catalo.'

In May of 1887, Jones began his second attempt to capture buffalo calves. This expedition was chronicled by the distinguished western writer Emerson Hough and illustrated by J. A. Ricker.[63] Hough, who had never seen a buffalo, saw this as the "last chance" to see this emblematic animal of the western plains. He and his companion were going to "learn something definite about these representatives of a grand and passing race." Jones made this a unique western experience for Hough. Coffee beans were ground in a buffalo skull, a buffalo shoulder was used as a shovel, a stove was made out of the brain cavity of a buffalo skull, buffalo chips were used for fuel, and one of Jones' exhausted and dehydrated Kentucky mares drank a pint of Kentucky whiskey out of a pail. This was a world unknown to easterners such as Hough and Ricker, and although Jones laid it on a bit heavy, the writer and illustrator could not help but be impressed by Jones' frontier skills. To solve the problem of feeding the calves once they were separated from their mothers, Jones brought with him twelve cows to nurse the young captives. While it may have been a good idea, in actual practice, the buffalo calves usually would not nurse from the cows. The problem of feeding them remained and would be a persistent issue on all of his calf catching expeditions. Of the fourteen calves captured, only seven were alive by the time they reached Jones' ranch on the banks of the Arkansas River.

Jones, naturally, was seeking to profit from these endeavors. In a city that was built by boosters, Jones' entrepreneurial activities were always noticed, if not always approved. In the fall of 1887, the *Garden City Herald* reported that "C. J. Jones has just received a letter from Buffalo Bill, who is now exhibiting his wildwest show in London, in which he offers him one thousand dollars apiece for his entire herd of buffalo."

"Pawnee Bill" Lilley , "Buffalo Bill" Cody, and
"Buffalo" Jones studio portrait (circa 1909)

If Mr. Jones sees fit to accept the offer he could clean up over forty thousand dollars on this little outside flyer. He went into the business of catching and domesticating buffalo, not as a matter of business, but as an amusement, and for the purpose of demonstrating a theory he held in regard to the hardy character of the cross between the buffalo and blooded stock. His buffalo have become more valuable by far than he ever expected." [65]

"Pawnee Bill" Lilley ,"Buffalo Bill" Cody, and
"Buffalo" Jones studio portrait (circa 1909)

In the spring of 1888 and 1889, Jones again organized calf capturing expeditions. The 1888 expedition lasted from April 20th to July 6th and was the most substantial and successful of his efforts to acquire buffalo calves. Jones expended $1825 and captured thirty-two calves. Jones' activities on the southern plains were now known throughout the nation and, in May of 1889, he began his last buffalo hunt. The progress of this expedition was to be carried by the Chicago Times. The Times provided Jones with carrier pigeons with which to send   dispatches from the scene of the hunt. Galloway cows were taken along to nurse the calves. On each hunt fewer and fewer wild buffalo had been seen. Leaving Garden City for the headwaters of the Canadian River in the Pan handle of Texas, he hoped to encounter a herd of at least twenty-five or thirty buffalo and then round them up and drive them north. The difficulty of driving a herd of buffalo was well known. Of the twenty-one they captured, only seven calves safely reached his ranch. The financial dimension of these expeditions are unclear, and how Jones raised expenses and profited from these endeavors is not recorded. While there was a market for live buffalo, it surely must have been a rather small market. Nevertheless, the Garden City Weekly Herald reported on March 13, 1890 that the "Hon. C. J. Jones sold a pair of buffalo to Mr. Bass, president of the First National Bank of Fort Wayne, Indiana for "$1000. They were shipped last Saturday."

By 1891, Jones had a ranch with buffalo at McCook, Nebraska.[66] In September of that year, Jones offered to sell ten mature buffalo to a British nobleman. On October 19th, five pairs of bison were loaded on a stock car for delivery to the White Star Steamship Company docks in New York City. From there they were transported to Liverpool, England aboard the steamship *Runic*[67]. Safely delivering the cargo, Jones presented rugs woven from the hair of the buffalo to Sir Walter Gilbey, President of the Agricultural and Fat Stock Association of the British Isles and to His Royal Highness, the Prince of Wales.[68] In a letter acknowledging this gift, it was noted that the "Prince has always taken the greatest interest in the American buffalo, and agrees with you in regretting the wantonness of the slayers of such a noble race. His Royal Highness wishes you every success in the efforts you are making to reproduce this almost extinct race of animals."[69]

Seeking to expand his herd of buffalo, Jones purchased Major Sam Bedson's herd from Stony Mountain, Manitoba, Canada in the fall of 1889.

BUFFALO HERD OWNED BY JONES WHILE IN
GARDEN CITY, KANSAS (CIRCA 1886)

Inman claims that Jones paid $25,000 for this herd, but there is some debate not only as to how much was actually paid for these animals but also how many there were.[70] The numbers range from 93 to 127 buffalo.[71] While in Canada, Jones also acquired a moose calf which he bought back to Kansas and ultimately sold to a park at Hutchinson, Kansas.[72]

At his ranch in Garden City, Jones now had one hundred and thirty-five buffalo, an undisclosed number of which he said he shipped to Salt Lake City, Utah and sold. In Kansas, he began to experiment with cross breeding buffalo by mating male buffalo with domestic cows. He named the animals that resulted from such breeding the catalo.

CATALO — JONES' EXPERIMENT IN CROSS BREEDING
THE MALE BUFFALO WITH DOMESTIC COWS.

His breeding experiments gave him the opportunity to not only learn about these hybrids but also about the most effective way of maintaining domesticated buffalo. Indeed, he gives the most detailed and complete description of how buffalo can be kept and handled that can be found for this period.[73] Using a five or six strand barb wire fence, he maintained fifty to one hundred buffalo on a section of land for a year.

By 1898, he estimated that there were approximately five hundred domesticated buffalo throughout the world; many of whom could trace their ancestry back to animals captured by him. He bred them with Galloways,

Angus, and Herefords. While he was determined to develop the catalo, he was also committed to preserving the surviving remnants of the great herds that once roamed freely.

In 1887, Jones traveled to Washington seeking support from the Kansas representatives in the House and Senate to preserve the small herds remaining in southeastern Colorado and the Pan handle of Texas. Little success attended this lobbying effort. Nevertheless, for the balance of his life, he frequently presented petitions to Congress for the preservation of the buffalo. In 1896, he proposed to Hoke Smith, the Secretary of Interior, that he be appointed with the authority to preserve the buffalo in Yellowstone National Park.[74] No action was taken. After President McKinley's inauguration in 1897, he proposed to the First Assistant Secretary of the Interior that he be given responsibility for the buffalo in Yellowstone National Park with the authority "to corral the remaining band, and thereby reproduce a herd that every true American will be proud of."[75]

Rather than face another rejection on proposals to save the diminishing buffalo herds in Yellowstone, Jones proposed to Congress in 1900 that he be leased 20,000 acres of the public domain in southwestern New Mexico for a period of twenty years. On this land, he would place his herd of buffalo. While sheep and cattle ranchers were using the land for free, Jones offered to pay an annual rent of one cent per acre. He would maintain his herd and make improvements on the land at his own expense. As well as maintaining a pure herd of buffalo, he would also conduct experiments in cross-breeding. Not only would the government be given an annual rent, but it would also receive each year two buffalo for the national parks. The proposal had the support of Senator Baker of Kansas and Representative John Lacey of Iowa in the House. Jones tried to rally public support for his proposal by giving frequent interviews to the press. The *Mail and Breeze* on February 17, 1900 carried such an interview. "Any man with American blood in his veins," he said," must be in sympathy with a plan to preserve the only American animal of domestic utility . . . The land which I want congress to set apart for twenty-five years for this purpose lies in the extreme southwestern corner of New Mexico and is about the size of Yellowstone National Park – that is about 3,300 square miles."[76] Jones made the case that this was only a small portion of the 33,000,000 unoccupied acres in New Mexico. Pedro Perea, the delegate from New Mexico, "stated before the committee that the buffalo and the Indian are things of the past and should have been exterminated long ago."[77] Although a reasonable proposal, if the government was committed to preserving the buffalo, it was rejected in both 1900 and 1901.

By 1902, President Theodore Roosevelt was concerned about the fate of

the buffalo, and at his urging, Congress appropriated $15,000 for the establish-
ment of a new buffalo herd at Yellowstone. At that time it was estimated that
there were between twenty-five and fifty buffalo in the park. The maintenance
of this herd became the park's principal annual appropriation.[78]

On July 8, 1902, Jones was commissioned Game Warden in Yellowstone
National Park at an annual salary of $1800.[79] Roosevelt's role in the
appointment of Jones is unclear.[80] Of all of those who played a role in the
preservation of the buffalo by capturing calves and developing small herds, Jones
is the only one who ever gains position with the federal government. A corral
to hold the herd was constructed about a mile from Mammoth Hot Spring.
Eighteen buffalo cows were purchased from the Allard herd in Montana and
three bulls from the Goodnight herd in Texas.[81] Major John Pitcher, Acting
Superintendent of the park, soon became estranged from Jones and his
erratic and solitary behavior.

Once the herd was established, Jones pursued more active adventures in
the park. In the spring of 1903, he sought to capture buffalo calves, pursued
mountain lions with his hounds, roped them, and brought them back to camp
on the back of his horse, and captured bears at the park's garbage dumps in a
rope snare.[82] Seeking to make the bears afraid of humans, he lifted the bears off
the ground with ropes hung from a tree and tied to their rear feet. He then
sought to intimidate them by switching them, prodding them with poles, and
firing blanks at them. Jones even made a motion picture of his spanking a
grizzly bear with a long pole, a scene which William T. Hornaday said always
elicited roars of laughter when shown.[83] Major Pitcher did not believe that Jones'
avoidance conditioning worked.[84] While a favorite with the park's tourists, Jones
became alienated from the soldiers and park staff whose support he needed. He
frequently criticized the language and drinking behavior of soldiers and the
management of the park. Jones resigned his position in September of 1905.

Although he was no longer Game Warden at Yellowstone, Jones still
sought federal support for his buffalo breeding experiments. With the approval
of Washington, he was given permission to survey remote areas beyond the north
rim of the Grand Canyon as a possible game preserve. On the Kaibab Plateau,
in an area that had not known buffalo in the historic period, Jones found a site
where he could implement his breeding program. Jones was once more a
boomer, an entrepreneur, a dreamer; and he sold his vision to two colleagues.
Stock would be issued, buffalo and catalo would be raised, profits would roll in.
In 1906, President Roosevelt established the Kaibab Plateau as the Grand
Canyon National Game Preserve.[85] With terms similar to those Jones had
proposed earlier to the government when he sought land for a buffalo park, a

concession was granted by the Secretary of Agriculture. One hundred black Galloway cows from Kansas would be mated with buffalo bulls for cross-breeding. Buffalo were acquired from the Goodnight Ranch in Texas and a ranch in Monterey, California. Getting the buffalo from the railhead to the preserve was a difficult task, and his success in getting most of them to the plateau speaks to his ability to work with wild animals. The buffalo bred easily, but difficulties in successfully crossbreeding buffalo bulls and the cows created dilemmas. Male calves often aborted or took the life of the cow. Heifer calves from the first breeding could be bred back to buffalo, but they produced sterile male calves.[86] At times Jones, who was occasionally referred to in the press as the "Animal Burbank," had dreams of crossbreeding still other species. In a presentation at the annual meeting of the American Breeders Association on January 16, 1907, he even contemplated crossing domestic sheep with antelopes to give them the swiftness to escape predators. At one point, he wished to cross Rocky Mountain Bighorns with Persian sheep to create a larger, wool producing sheep and with the hardiness to withstand the ardors of winter. Limited in his knowledge of animal genetics, he was always thinking of animal crosses that could live in arid, wind swept western lands, or Alaska, and produce the wool, hides, milk, or meat that could be marketed. He also experimented with crosses between Persian and Merino sheep to create what he called "Perserinoes."

5

Pursuit of the Musk Ox

T he most arduous experience that Jones ever endured was his 1897-1898 trip to the Arctic to capture musk oxen, "the most remote animal of the world," and the only mega fauna which had not yet been placed in captivity.[87] Members of *Bovidae*, these ruminants were in the same family as bison and domestic cattle. Often referred as the "bison of the tundra," musk oxen bulls were smaller than bison and seldom exceeded 800 pounds in weight. Found in herds of up to 100, they were singularly adapted to life in high latitudes. While bison could endure the blizzards of the plains, musk oxen with their double coat of hair survived in the more challenging environment of the Arctic. Jones remarked that his "mission was to bring out from the Arctic regions musk-oxen alive, if possible; and also silver-gray fox, marten, and other valuable fur bearing animals, to propagate on an island in the Pacific ocean."[88] Leaving Perry, Oklahoma, Jones embarked on a journey of four hundred and ninety-five days. Traveling by train to Edmonton, Canada, he acquired those items he would need for his expedition. A rubber life preserver, shoes with steel calks, bull-rings for the noses of captured musk-oxen, traps of all kinds, and shepherd dogs were obtained. For the lengthy journey that was planned, he purchased 1500 pounds of flour and 400 pounds of bacon, beans, rice, oat-meal, coffee, tea, and sugar. In the tradition of prospectors who raced to the Klondike and Yukon, he built his own boat, 25 feet in length and 9 feet wide, along the shores of the Athabaska River. Traveling in this boat, Jones experienced the same dangers from river rapids that had become common to those who raced to the north for gold. Encountering Chippewas, Crees, and Slaves, Jones ineffectively attempted to explain his plans to capture musk-oxen. With three companions, Jones was determined to be successful in this venture, but experienced northern travelers predicted failure. "I was told all along the route by Hudson Bay

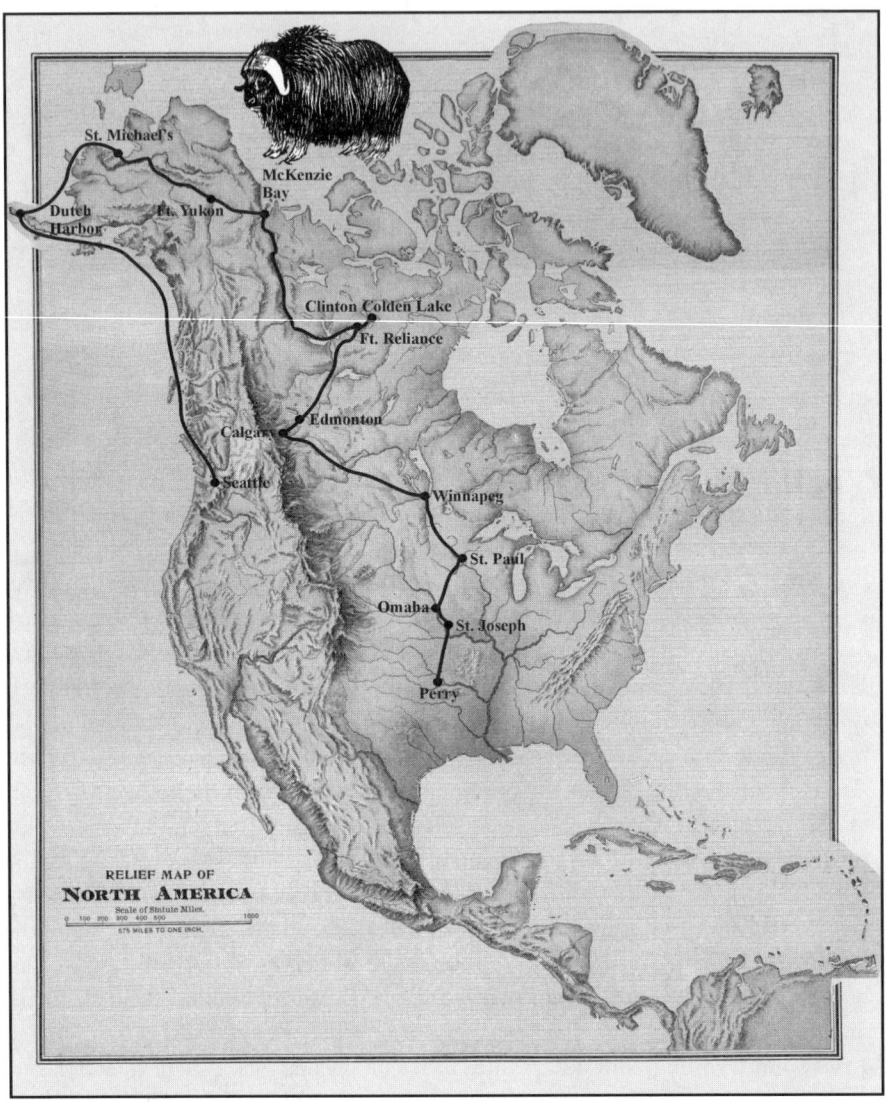

ITINERARY OF JONES' TRIP TO THE ARCTIC (1897-98) TO CAPTURE MUSK OXEN.

traders that I would never take a musk-ox out of the northern country, and that I was only wasting my time to attempt it, for the Indians would never help me in the least. More than that, if I did get any, the Indians would kill them alive."[89] By the 16th of November, the hunt for musk oxen began, but they learned that the animals were still too far to the north. It is during this expedition that Jones has his most extensive experience with native Americans.[90] The impoverished native peoples of the north with their constant demands for food, clothing, tools, and weapons were a challenge to Jones and his companions. On the 28th of February, 1898, they left their base camp near Ft. Reliance, in the Northwest Territories. By early March, although plagued nightly by Arctic wolves, they had taken their first musk oxen. When Jones began to skin out these animals, he sensed immediately their primary anatomical uniqueness; and any dream he harbored of crossing them with cattle or buffalo disappeared.[91] Ultimately, Jones captured five musk oxen calves, surely the first calves ever to have been lassoed and hog tied.[92] Through the nine hours of darkness which occurred during the first night after the capture of the calves, Jones and his companion fought off a pack of wolves which sensed an easy meal. Twelve wolves were killed, and twice that number wounded.[93]

Although Jones had captured his calves, the task of bringing them to civilization lay ahead of him. Four days later, after taking a rest break, they awoke to find that the five calves had had their throats cut. "There had been twelve or fifteen Eskimos or Indians there on snowshoes, and they had cut the throats of all of our animals. . . We had been warned time and time again by the Indians not to take any musk-oxen alive. . .We abandoned all hope of securing even a single live musk-ox. We would have returned to their haunts and tried again, but knew that such action would be suicidal, as our ammunition was almost gone; it was a serious question whether we could reach our cabin without taking great chances of starvation."[94]

The dilemma confronting Jones was to determine the safest way of returning to civilization. As he planned his withdrawal from these high northern latitudes, he contemplated what experiences and strength of character would be necessary to reach the North Pole. "After my experiences in the Far North, I have come to the conclusion that the man who reaches the North Pole must be made of sterner metal than anyone who thus far has attempted the perilous journey. No 'tenderfoot' will ever hang the flag of his country on the mythical pole, or on a real one, at the northern extremity of this terrestrial globe. When I say 'tenderfoot,' I mean anyone who has not experience in all the arts required to meet every contingency necessary to such an undertaking."[95] Jones surely felt that after his months of experience pursing the musk-ox that he was no tenderfoot. To reach the North Pole, Jones believed that one essential attribute was necessary. "I refer to the will-power and willingness to do or die, without which the explorer will fail in his purpose."[96] Ultimately, Jones elects to return to the United States by way of Alaska. After traveling down the Yukon River, through the Aleutians, with a stop at St. Michael's and Dutch Harbor, he arrives in Seattle on October 6th, 1898.

In a life filled with adventure and outdoor experiences that have not yet been chronicled in the detail that they might, Jones and his daughter had an experience seldom equaled in the Rocky Mountains. Jones accepted a commission from the Secretary of the Smithsonian Institution to capture a Big Horn Sheep for the National Zoological Park in Washington. In May of 1900, Jones received permission from the Governor of Colorado to capture a dozen of these animals. *Harper's Weekly* describes this endeavor in some detail. Accompanied by his daughter, Olive, and Charles Smith, a local Norwegian who guided parties on the Western Slope of the Rockies, Jones set up camp near Redstone, Colorado on the Crystal River. In a region of towering mountains and majestic alpine beauty, Jones began his quest. At timber line, they often searched for their breath as well as the elusive mountain sheep. Full grown rams were seen, but approached with difficulty. Ewes with their lambs were more elusive, and it was not until the middle of May, 1900 that they found a lamb abandoned by its mother in a talus slope. Olive had seen the mother hide it among the gray rocks and then scamper away. With two half-hitches in his rope, Jones lowered his daughter down among the boulders and the ewe was captured. Placed in a gunny sack with its head sticking out, the young sheep was carried to a small community at the base of the mountain near Avalanche Creek to be nourished while other animals were captured. With much effort another lamb was caught, and with much enthusiasm both lambs were nursed from bottles. His daughter took a particular interest in these animals and soon had them performing a variety of feats at her command. Impressed by agility of these animals, Jones was seeking a domestic animal with which to cross breed them.

6

Zane Grey and Buffalo Jones: The Creation of a Western Author

In early 1907, Zane Grey, then a struggling author who had recently abandoned a career as a dentist, met Buffalo Jones in New York City.[97] Grey occasionally attended meetings of the Camp Fire Club, a prominent turn of the century wildlife and conservation organization. At this club, he had become friends with Alvah James, a South American explorer. James invited Grey to a public lecture and film presentation given by Buffalo Jones. The audience did not respond well to Jones' presentation and film believing that his stories of his western wildlife experiences – roping rattlesnakes, buffalo and mountain lions, crossing buffalo and cattle – exceeded the credulity of eastern listeners. Some cat called, others hissed, some walked out. Jones was angered and embarrassed. Nevertheless, Grey was captivated by Jones and his experiences and sought to meet Jones. Meeting Jones in his hotel room, Grey expressed his interest in learning more of his attempts to breed the catalo. He then told Jones that he would like to return to Arizona with him to gather material for a book on Jones and his attempts at buffalo hybridization. This book would popularize Jones' endeavors and make it easier for him to raise support for his programs. Initially skeptical of the young man's talents, Jones asked Grey if he could write. Grey gave him a copy of his *Betty Zane*; and when Jones read that work, he agreed to Grey's joining him in Arizona.[98]

In Arizona, Jones met Zane Grey on the north rim of the Grand Canyon, and so imprinted Grey with a love of the West and its heroic figures that The *Last of the Plainsmen* became in effect a chronicle of the more memorable episodes in Jones' life.

BOOK COVER RENDITION OF ZANE GREY'S *LAST OF THE PLAINSMEN*.

Grey describes his initial encounter with Jones. "In the spring of 1907, I was the fortunate companion of the old plainsman on a trip across the desert, and a hunt in that wonderful country of yellow crags, deep canons and giant pines. Never shall I forget the color and beauty of those painted cliffs and the long, brown-matted, bluebell-dotted aisles in the grand forests, the tang of the dry, cool air. They will ever be associated in my mind with the life and nature of that strange character and remarkable man, Buffalo Jones."[99] While the initial plan was to portray Jones' work in cross breeding buffalo and cattle, a more adventuresome story arose with Jones and the party chasing and roping mountain lions.

JONES WITH HUNTING DOGS ON THE GRAND CANYON ADVENTURE.

After the death of Jones, Grey remarked that "Buffalo Jones was great in all the remarkable qualities common to the men who opened the West. No doubt something of Buffalo Jones crept unconsciously into all of the great fictional characters I have created."[100] Grey witnessed not only the splendor of the Canyon country for the first time but also viewed the awesome splendor of the Colorado River. Jones figures prominently not only in The *Last of the Plainsmen* and *Roping Lions in the Grand Canyon*, but also appears, or is mentioned, in *Raiders of Spanish Peaks*, *Shadow on the Trail*, and *The Thundering Herd*. The *Last of the Plainsmen* portrays Jones as a moral exemplar for Americans. No men are killed in this work, and curiously, perhaps to emphasize Grey's perception of the manliness and maleness of the West, no woman is mentioned.

CHARLES J. JONES

MCM XI

DRAWN BY ALBERT OPERTI

"BUFFALO" JONES AND A FEW OF HIS CAPTIVES

NINTH ANNUAL DINNER

OF THE

CANADIAN CAMP

HOTEL ASTOR, NEW YORK

MARCH SIXTH

1911

PROGRAM COVER OF AN EVENT IN NEW YORK CITY (1911).

As he entered his mid-sixties and time began to take its natural toll on his physical stamina, Jones devoted more time to lecturing and showing slides and motion pictures of buffalo and the wildlife of the American West and Africa than he did to actually working with buffalo or pursuing breeding experiments. His income came from the public lectures that he gave for a variety of lecture bureaus. The last adventures of Jones' life were his African trips of 1910 and 1914.

BUFFALO JONES

"THE MAN WHO DOES THINGS"
JOHN D. ROCKFELLER, Jr.

AND

Teaches Others How to do Them

"The boy at 70."
W. H. THOMPSON,
U. S. Senator.

"The real Daniel."
Governor ROSCO STUBBS.

"The American hero."
ELBERT HUBBARD.

"The Burbank of the
animal kingdom."
JAMES WILSON,
Ex-Secretary of Agriculture.

"The practical
naturalist."
VIC MURDOCK, M.C.

"The cowboy poet."
General NELSON MILES.

"The greatest
humanitarian."
Miss LOTTA CRABTREE,
America's Greatest Actress.

"KING OF COWBOYS."
W. F. CODY, (Buffalo Bill)

"America never produced a more adventur=
ous and daring a man than Buffalo Jones"
WM. T. HORNADAY,
Brightest authority on Wild Animals.

He also teaches

Knowledge,

Wisdom,

Self Reliance,

Humanity,

Brotherly Love,

Virtue,

Honor,

Justice

and

Mercy.

"Buffalo Jones' work with wild animals is beyond anything ever recorded in the
annals of time. My hunt sinks into insignificance compared with it."
Ex-President THEODORE ROOSEVELT.

"Your lecture gave me more to think about than any I ever listened to."
DR. HADLEY, President of Yale College.

"Teach the boys to be like Buffalo Jones, the Ideal Scout of the World."
BADEN POWELL.

"All Travelogue Lecturers take their hats off to Buffalo Jones."
BURTON HOLMES.

"Unbelievable without seeing the proof in pictures and hearing Buffalo Jones'
lecture."
Ex-President WILLIAM H. TAFT.

At_____

BROOKLYN EAGLE PRESS.

ADVERTISING POSTER FOR BUFFALO JONES' LECTURES AND SLIDE SHOWS.

7

The African Expeditions of Buffalo Jones

Jones' 1910 safari to East Africa, and the motion picture that he made of his roping African game, kept his name before the American public and gave him additional topics for his lecture series.[101] In 1909, Jones escorted Charles S. Bird, a friend of Zane Grey and a successful Massachusetts industrialist, on a mountain lion hunt on the Kaibab Plateau. Around the campfire on the northern rim of the Grand Canyon, they discussed Theodore Roosevelt's recent, and widely covered, 1909 African safari. In the course of that 1909 expedition, Roosevelt had taken more than five hundred big game animals and six hundred lesser animals. Roosevelt justified this carnage by proclaiming that they were collected for museums and scientific collections. Deploring the killing of wild animals, Jones suggested that he thought that it would be possible to lasso all of the animals that Roosevelt had shot.[102] The publication of Roosevelt's African GameTrails in 1910 further piqued Jones' interest in such an expedition. Jones simply wanted to capture and release many of the same animals that Roosevelt had shot. Indeed, he even contemplated branding lions with the brand "BJ" to show that Buffalo Jones had captured and released them. Fortunately, this branding was never done. The expedition would be funded by Charles S. Bird and would have as its goal not only the roping of the major game animals of East Africa but also the production of a motion picture film which would chronicle their activities. Guy Scull suggests that there was still another motive for the trip. "They were really going to try and find some African big game to bring back to the Western U.S.A. for crossing with buffalo in experiments to produce a new hybrid that would provide both hide and meat at low cost for the market."[103]

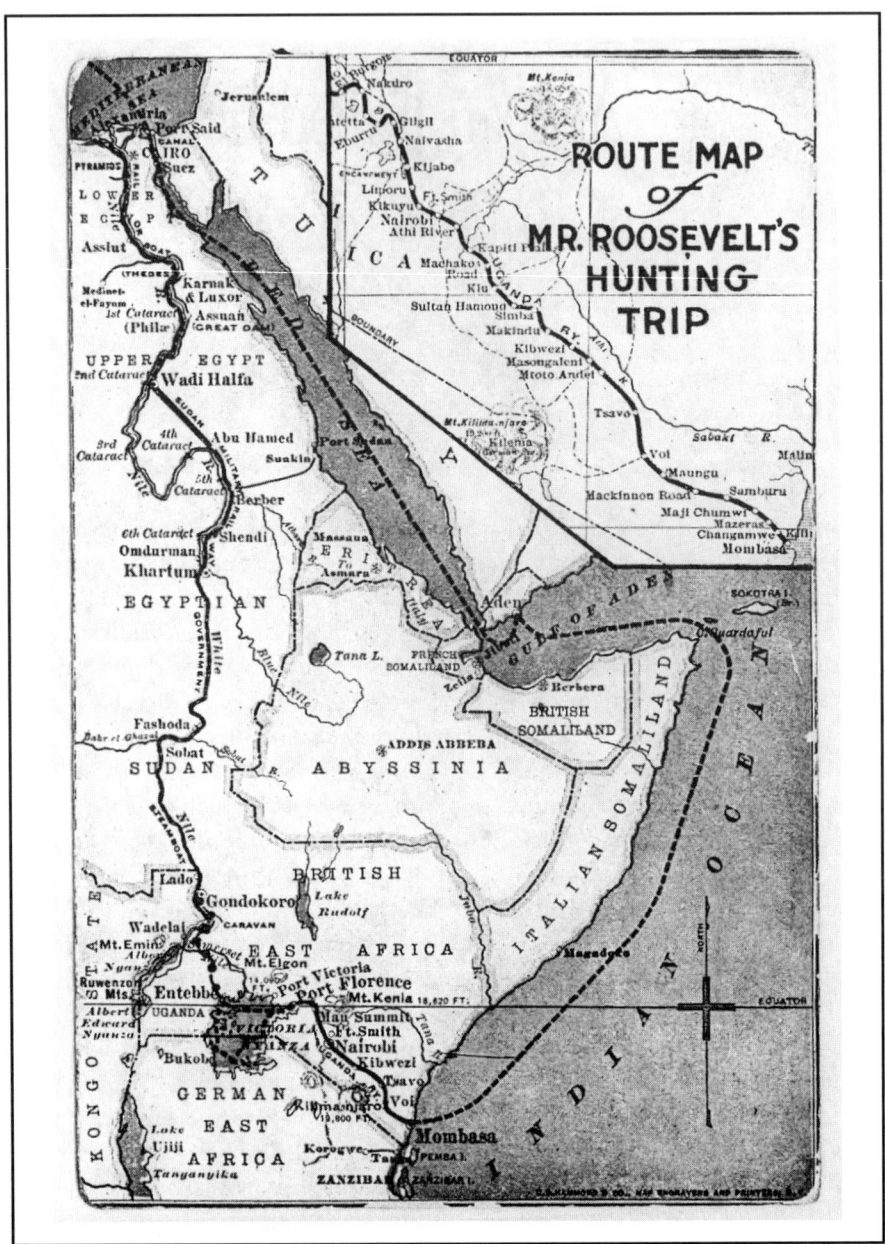

MAP OF THEODORE ROOSEVELT'S 1909 AFRICAN SAFARI, SAID
TO HAVE BEEN THE SAME ROUTE JONES FOLLOWED IN 1910.

Even in his later years, after many disappointments in his breeding experiments, Jones could not stop thinking of animals that he might cross breed in order to acquire more useful and desirable qualities for human use. Even the musk ox with its remarkably fine hair had been a candidate for cross breeding. The lassoing of African animals would be done by Buffalo Jones and two cowboys – Marshall Loveless from Kansas and New Mexico and Ambrose Means from Arizona.

COLONEL JONES (CENTER) AND LOVELESS AND MEANS ON
AFRICAN SAFARI TO ROPE WILD ANIMALS IN 1910.

The photographer for the expedition was the experienced English naturalist and photographer, Cherry Kearton. Kearton had also made a brief film of some of Roosevelt's African exploits. Jones was experienced with a lasso but not with making films, and conflict quickly arose over how the animals of East Africa could be roped and how the filming of the lassoing of a animal could be accomplished. Kearton wanted the animals roped at specified sites before a pre-positioned camera. Jones was not sure that wild animals could be found and then easily driven to those sites where they would be filmed when the light was best.

Daily details of the expedition were to be handled by Guy Scull, a graduate of Harvard and a member of Roosevelt's Rough Riders.[104] Other members of the expedition were Kearton's assistant, David Gobbet, and Ray Ulyate, an experienced East African hunter. Accompanying the expedition as well were twelve cow ponies and twenty-one dogs, —four from Jones' pack in Arizona and seventeen from England. There were many who doubted that

African animals could be lassoed, hog-tied, muzzled, and then handled by man; but then they could not appreciate Jones' demonstrated talents for roping rattlesnakes, buffalo calves, grizzly bears, and musk oxen. Still, one correspondent posed the question, "What will happen after he has lassoed them he does not pretend to say; that is a secret between the lion and Mr. Jones and Scull."[105] Jones replied that he would have photographs made to show what he had done.

The expedition sailed from Southhampton for Aden and then through the Suez Canal to Mombasi on February 3rd, and then on to Nairobi by train. Arriving there by March 3, 1910, they learned that Theodore Roosevelt had just recently killed a large rhinoceros in the very area to which they were headed. To hold an animal as large a rhino and as fierce as lion, Jones, Loveless, and Means were using lassoes of hard-twisted Russian hemp no thicker than a little finger. They believed that their lassoes would hold up to two tons. Once a large animal was captured, they were planning to tie it down with a rope that had a steel wire in its center.[106] When they left Nairobi in the traditional safari parade, they were accompanied by 135 native porters. The logistics of the expedition were complex and expensive.

PARADE THROUGH NAIROBI WITH JONES IN FRONT.

Jones had withstood the rigors of travel on the plains, the dangers of the Colorado River and the Grand Canyon, the harsh and frigid conditions of the Arctic, but he had not yet confronted the debilitating heat and pestilent conditions found in the Kedong and Rift valleys. In the course of this expedition, Jones, Means, Loveless and their dogs and horses all became ill from African diseases. With one rider serving as a header and the two other riders acting as heelers, they demonstrated that lesser African game could be lassoed and captured. "Cheetah, eland, hartebeest, and serval-cat were roped and tied and photographed." After much crossing of the veldt, they finally came across a giraffe which they successfully lassoed, tied, and photographed.[107]

ROPING A GIRAFFE IN AFRICA.

To really demonstrate their skills as western cowboys, they needed to rope an elephant or rhino. No elephant was found, but they did encounter a white rhino. While the photographers had some trepidations about attempting to hold such a large animal with a small hemp lariat, Jones, Means, and Loveless had none. Scull described this event in a letter to Henry Case. "The Colonel and the cowboys roped him and fought him for five hours in the hot sunlight before he was beaten . It was a little, very little like playing a large fish on a light line. In the beginning, the rhino dragged the horses all about, even though the horses planted their four feet firmly on the ground, as they are trained to do with cattle; but in the end the horses dragged the rhino – dragged him to a clump of thorn trees, where the cowboys tied him, properly heeled, with all the ropes at hand. Once, the Colonel was nearly caught. There was scarcely daylight between his horse's tail and the up thrust of the rhino's head."[108]

JONES ROPING THE RHINO IN AFRICA.

In exceptionally rough terrain of lava blocks, broken ground, thorn trees, and thick shrub, the dogs bayed a lioness. The lioness broke from this region after being chased from one inaccessible spot to another by the throwing of fireworks onto the African plain. Jones, Loveless, and Means pursued it. Finally, after much difficulty, the lion was roped and held by a hind leg. Further secured,

JONES CAPTURING A LIONESS IN AFRICA.

she was placed on a cradle and pulled by horses into camp. This tableaux of events is captured on Kearton's film.

Ultimately, this lion was presented to William T. Hornaday, Director of the New York Zoological Society, and placed in the Bronx Zoo in New York City on June 15, 1910. On its 261 acres and under the direction of Hornaday, this zoo

JONES PRESENTING THE LIONESS TO THE BRONX ZOO
IN NEW YORK CITY ON JUNE 15, 1910.

became the world's exemplar for the exhibition of living wildlife. The lioness lived for another eleven years. In commenting upon this gift, Hornaday, who had been skeptical of Jones' African trip, remarked "I was never proved wrong in a fashion I liked better. I've been one of your strongest admirers since you caught those buffalo in the prairie thirty years ago, and I now accept your gift of the East African lioness, taken by the Buffalo Jones Expedition in Kenya. So far as I know, it's the first lioness ever caught by a man 65 years old riding a New Mexico cowpony wielding a grass rope."[109] At the conclusion of Jones' expedition and upon the publication of Guy H. Scull's *Lassoing Wild Animals in Africa* 1911, Theodore Roosevelt graciously commented that "No hunting trip more worthy of commemoration ever took place in Africa." [110]

PROMOTIONAL POSTER ENDORSED BY FORMER PRESIDENT ROOSEVELT.

Exhausted by the rigors of this expedition and disappointed by his failure to rope an elephant, Jones returned to popular acclaim and many opportunities to lecture.

Nevertheless, the financial rewards which he expected from this arduous trip failed to materialize. Jones always wanted to "see the elephant," to know what lay over the next hill, to have one more moment of success after a challenging adventure. In September 1913, he wrote a poignant letter seeking support for another African trip. This time he wished to capture a gorilla and bring it back alive to the United States. After the salutation, Jones addressed the request poetically:

> "The call of the wild I've heard again,
>   As it echoes over the sea,
> It's as clear as the tom-tom's thrilling note,
>   Calling the braves to revelry.
> The call I heard when a boy of twelve,
>   And again at twelve times three
> Each time I obeyed and reaped rewards,
>   More precious than gold to me.
> The summons is one I always obey,
>   One my soul can never deny,
> And the beasts may resolve, again and again,
>   They are masters, endowed from on high.
> But I am as sure as sure can be,
>   Will stake my life on conquering all;
> So bring my horse, saddle and rope,
>   And I will answer the call."

> "How would you like to go with me to Africa?
> I am after gorillas and other big game.
>   Sincerely yours,
>   — C.J. Jones[111]"

The poem above was sent to Arthur Mougey of Youngstown, Ohio who raised $8,500 for this expedition. He and his wife would accompany Jones on his expedition to the Congo, but in the course of this most arduous expedition, serious disagreements developed between Jones and the Mougeys.

No one had yet successfully captured and kept alive a gorilla, and the methods for doing this were much debated. African folk tales told of the fondness that gorillas had for music and for women. Jones, thinking that this might be true, brought with him a phonograph player and two women. To the tunes of "I Dream Of Jeannie With The Light Brown Hair" or "Believe Me If All

Those Endearing Young Charms," the gorilla was to be lured into a trap and captured. Mrs. Ambrose Means, a champion rodeo rider with distinctive feminine charms, was to calm the captured, savage beast by her presence and soothing manner. Things did not work out as planned.

Preparations were made in London once more for an African trip. At a dog market in East London, he acquired nine Airedales to join the other eight dogs Jones had obtained for this expedition. By April of 1914, the party of Jones, the Mogueys, and Ambrose Means and his wife, had arrived at Cape Lopez. The bay was so shallow that all horses, supplies, and dogs had to be off loaded into smaller surf boats. When the Means' horses struggled in the hammock held by the hoist that was to place them in the smaller boats, the Means mounted their horses and were then lowered into surf. Jones captured this scene on film, but all of the film of this expedition has been lost.

From Cape Lopez, the party moved to a base camp on the shore of Lake Fernan-Vaz. When no gorillas were found, they established another camp below Lake N'Gove. Moving deeper into the jungle, they at last encountered gorillas. They were unsuccessful in capturing one of these animals, but they did kill an adult male and female.

The demands of jungle travel weakened the seventy year old Jones, and he came down with jungle fever. Wracked with malaria, plagued with exhaustion, and then debilitated by heart problems, the second African expedition had to be abandoned. Jones never recovered from the weakened condition in which he left Africa in October of 1914.

8

The End of Life

In the last years of his life, Jones moved frequently. Leaving his ranch at Portales, New Mexico, he lived briefly at San Antonio and Denver. At both locations, ever the promoter, he sought support to market a patented irrigation device which he had invented. In his last years, he returned to the passion of his younger years, bringing and distributing water to the lands of the arid west.[112]

In his last years, Charles Jesse Jones
with grandson, Charles R. Whitmer.

Jones' successes and failures in his life were in a large measure a coefficient of his personality. By nature abstemious, he avoided coffee, tea, and liquor and led a disciplined personal life. He discouraged profanity and seldom used even the most mild of frontier profanities. Blessed with a way with words, he was an effective public speaker who captured the attention of audiences with graphic descriptions of his experiences upon the plains, in the frozen Arctic, along the rim of the Grand Canyon, in the veldt of East Africa or the dense jungles of the Congo. Although accused by many of exaggerations, his tall tales usually had a basis in truth. He was as comfortable around a buffalo chip campfire as he was in the presence of a President of the United States.

While frequently away from home, his personal life was exemplary, although marked by personal tragedy. His love for his wife was unquestioned, and he was moved visibly by her death in 1907. Two young sons died during the fourteen years he lived at Garden City. Two daughters had died earlier while he lived at Sterling, Kansas. His two remaining daughters, Olive and Jessie, were always in his thoughts, and they corresponded frequently with their father.

JONES'DAUGHTER, OLIVE, AND WIFE, MARTHA, POSE AT THE
JONES FAMILY RESIDENCE AT 515 N. NINTH IN GARDEN CITY, KANSAS.

He died on October 14, 1919 and was buried in a simple grave in Garden City, Kansas. The fourteen years that he spent at Garden City were an essential part of his life's experiences.

By the time of his death, the buffalo had been saved from extinction. Jones' contributions to the preservation of the buffalo are more significant than his cross-breeding experiment to create the catalo. While he sought to profit from his commitment to their preservation, he was sincere in his desire to prevent them from becoming extinct. Although his role as a wildlife photographer has not been defined, in lecture after lecture, in city after city, he presented motion pictures and lantern slides of the Yellowstone buffalo and lion hunting in the Grand Canyon. Willing always to take credit for a development and given to self-promotion and overstatement, he should be acknowledged nevertheless for his persistence in bringing to Washington a frontier perspective on how the buffalo could be preserved. In his 1907 speech before the American Breeders Association, he observed that he had bred more than 1500 buffalo from 82 buffalo calves, 58 of which "I captured and saved with my own hands . . . consequently, I think that I have atoned for my part in the extermination to a great extent." His remarks and lantern slides were approved by a standing ovation and three cheers. All evidence suggests that he captured more wild buffalo than any of the other individuals in the last quarter of the nineteenth century. He was   dedicated to the preservation of the species. Clearly, there is no question about his investing more of his personal time, energy, and capital to their preservation than any other American. Most domesticated herds of the twentieth century bear within their members the genetic stamp of animals once owned or collected by Buffalo Jones.

CHARLES J. "BUFFALO" JONES

—Suggested Readings—

For those individuals who wish to learn more about the fascinating life of Buffalo Jones, the endnotes provide references to many of the diverse sources that speak to his career. The most informative source for his career is Henry Inman's publication of Jones' account of his life in *Buffalo Jones' Forty Years of Adventure* (Topeka: Crane and Company, 1899). An abridgment of this work appeared as *Buffalo Jones' Adventures on the Plains* (Lincoln: University of Nebraska Press, 1970). The following volumes also contribute to an understanding of his accomplishments: Robert Easton and Mackenzie Brown, *Lord of the Beasts, the Life of Buffalo Jones* (Lincoln: University of Nebraska Press, 1970). Zane Grey's *The Last of the Plainsmen* (many editions and publishers) provides a dramatic description of Grey's journey with Jones to the northern rim of the Grand Canyon in 1908. Details of Jones first African trip with illustrations may be found in Guy H. Scull's *Lassoing Wild Animals in Africa* (New York: Frederick A. Stokes Company, 1911).

—Acknowledgements—

With much gratitude, the Finney County Historical Society would like to acknowledge the substantial financial contribution that the Garden City, Kansas Rotary Club made to this project. Without that support, this book could not have been published at this time. President Blake Waters was particularly helpful in suggesting that this local history project was worthy to be designated as a Rotary International Centennial Project. Other Rotarians who were involved were Ron Isham, Troy Unruh and Bryce Baker.

The Society wishes to recognize the Kansas Humanities Council whose grant money enabled securing the services of author Phillip Thomas. The Society is also pleased to have contracted with artist Jerry Thomas for his original cover rendition of Buffalo Jones.

Finney County Historical Museum staff members Olga Montgomery, Jan Coulter and Todd Roberts contributed their research and computer expertise and took time away from other assignments to provide their assistance.

Judy Entz, Mennonite Press Consultant, and Mary Regan, Executive Director of the Finney County Historical Society, have been able mentors, guiding the project from beginning to end and acting as liaisons between all parties involved.

In addition, Charles R. Whitmer Jr. and Alexander Phillips, grandsons of C.J. Jones, have graciously shared oral history and artifacts belonging to their grandfather.

The Publication Committee members listed below have given tirelessly of their time and generously of their advice during the whole process of publishing this important work.

PUBLICATIONS COMMITTEE
Norman Clark, Carol Hodgkinson, Deb Jarmer,
Blanche Larson, Ruth Richards, and
Pat Fishback, Committee Chair

—Illustration Credits—

Most of the photos and illustrations in this book are from the collection of the Finney County Historical Society, with the following exceptions on pages indicated:

7   Sketch from Forty Years of Adventure by Col. Henry Inman;

31 & 32   Prints from the Finney County Historical Collection;

40   Map from a 1907 Scribner & Sons Atlas and musk ox drawing from *Lord of Beasts* by Easton &Brown (1961);

44   Book cover rendition of *Last of the Plainsmen* by Zane Grey;

45   Photo of Jones and his dogs from *Roping Lions In The Grand Canyon* by Zane Grey, published by Gosset and Dunlap (1922-24);

50   Postcard map of T. Roosevelt's trip to Africa from Phillip Thomas' collection;

51,52,53,54 Photos from *Lassoing Wild Animals in Africa* by Guy Scull, published by Frederick Stokes Co. (1911).

Endnotes

Introduction :

1   The details of Jones' participation in the attempts to settle on the Ute reservation are not well documented.

2   Colonel Henry Inman (compiler). *Buffalo Jones' Forty Years of Adventure*. (Topeka, Kansas: Crane & Company, 1899). Ralph T. Kersey's *Buffalo Jones, A True Biography* (Garden City, Kansas: Elliott Printers, 1958) and Robert Easton and Mackenzie Brown's *Lord of Beasts, The Life of Buffalo Jones* (1964) are based almost exclusively on this work. At times both works have almost the tone of an hagiography.

3   The Finney County Historical Society in Garden City, Kansas has a large collection of Jones' materials, but unfortunately most of his extensive correspondence is apparently no longer extant and the existence of the diaries and notes on which Inman based his work is unknown. Inman noted (p. xi) that Jones had "carefully kept" a journal of his diverse experiences.

4   Henry F. Mason, "County Seat Controversies in Southwestern Kansas," *Kansas Historical Quarterly*, Vol. II, No. 1, 1933, p. 46.

5   Apparently, the first use of the term "Buffalo" Jones in print does not appear until 1883. Other sources suggest that he began to be called "Buffalo" Jones because of his practices of displaying tamed buffalo at local fairs. Additional information on this battle and Jones role in may be found in John R. Crook's *The Border and the Buffalo*. Topeka: Crane and Co., 1907. Cook is a fascinating, but somewhat neglected figure in Kansas history. He served in Company E, 12th Kansas Infantry and patrolled the Kansas border against guerrilla incursions. At the end of the Civil War, he homesteaded 160 acres in Labette County and became its constable. In the fall of 1874, he began a career as a hide hunter in the Texas Panhandle. In the early 1880s, he became a temperance lecturer in Kansas. He died in 1917 at the Kansas Soldier's Home at Ft. Dodge. Cook implies that he participated in the Pocket Canyon Fight along with Pat Garrett. Zane Grey believed that Jones participated in this battle. Yet, given the enthusiasm with which Jones talked about his experiences, it is interesting to note that no description of this battle occurs in Inman nor does he make reference to it himself in any other written work. Given the many stories published about Jones in the press, it is curious that there is no other discussion of either how he got his name or this battle.

Chapter 1 : EARLY YOUTH AND CAREER OF CHARLES JESSE JONES

6   It is interesting to note that Jones grew up as a childhood friend of Elbert Hubbard the founder of the Roycrofters. Hubbard became one of the most popular writers and lecturers of the early 20th century and the founder of an arts and craft movement that emphasized simplicity of design, hand crafted quality, and celebration of human skills in the manufacture of daily items. Elbert Hubbard, *Pig-Pen Peter, or Some Chums of Mine*. (East Aurora: Roycrofters, 1914), p. 30.

7   *Pig-Pen Pete*, p.32

Chapter 2 : JONES FINDS HIS FUTURE UPON THE PLAINS

8   Inman, *Buffalo Jones*, p. 37

9   Inman, *Buffalo Jones*, p. 37

10   Blanchard, *Conquest of Southwest Kansas*, p. 229

Chapter 3 : BUFFALO JONES AND THE RISE OF GARDEN CITY

11   *The Garden City Paper*, May 8, 1879, p.14. Quotations from this paper are based upon *The Garden City Paper, A Reprinting of the Local News As It Happened in Garden City, Sequoyah County, Kansas, April 3, 1879-October 30, 1879, As Reported By Kirk Himrod and Amos Bain, Editors and Publishers* (Published by The William Wilson Chapter, Daughters of the American Revolution, 1976, Garden City, Finney County, Kansas. Hereinafter cited as *The Garden City Paper*.

12   *The Garden City Irrigator*, February 14, 1884

13   *The Garden City Paper*, May 22, 1879, p. 22

14   *The Garden City Irrigator*, December 11, 1884

15   *The Garden City Irrigator*, October 9, 1884

16   *The Garden City Irrigator*, December 12, 1885

17   *The Garden City Irrigator*, March 13, 1886

18   Leola Howard Blanchard, *Conquest of Southwest Kansas* (Leola Howard Blanchard:

The Wichita Eagle Press, 1931; Reprinted with additional notes and a new index, Finney County Historical Society, 1989), p. 239

19   *Garden City Irrigator*, April 19, 1883. Information from the *Garden City Irrigator* is taken from the Finney County Historical Society's *Topical Index to Newsworthy Events in the Garden City Irrigator*, 1882-1887 As Compiled by Katherine Kelley Powell, 1984.The Garden City Irrigator, April 16, 1883 Hereinafter cited as *The Garden City Paper*.

20   *The Garden City Irrigator*, April 16, 1883

21   *The Garden City Irrigator*, December 20, 1883

22   *The Garden City Irrigator*, June 26, 1884. During Major Stephen H. Long's 1819-1820 Expedition to the Rocky Mountain, the windswept, treeless, arid areas beyond the 100th Meridian began to be labeled the "Great American Desert," a land unsuitable for settlement. This concept of a Great American Desert was an impediment to western settlement.

23   *The Garden City Paper*, July 3, 1879, p.44

24   *The Garden City Paper*, July 3, 1879, p.45

25   *The Garden City Paper*, July 10, 1879, p.47

26   *The Garden City Paper*, July 3, 1879, p.43

27   *The Garden City Paper*, July 17, 1879, p.50

28   *The Garden City Paper*, July 31, 1879, p.57

29   *The Garden City Paper*, August 28, 1879, p.69

30   *The Garden City Paper*, September 18, 1879, p.83

31   *The Garden City Paper*, August 21, 1879, p.65

32   *The Garden City Paper*, August 21, 1879, p.67

33   *The Garden City Paper*, August 7, 1879, p.60

34   Blanchard, *Conquest of Southwest Kansas*, p.87-88

35   Blanchard, *Conquest of Southwest Kansas*, p. 95

36   Blanchard, *Conquest of Southwest Kansas*, p. 90

37   Blanchard, *Conquest of Southwest Kansas*, p. 91 quoting James Craig

38   Blanchard, *Conquest of Southwest Kansas*, p. 92 and *History of Kearny County Kansas*, Vol. I, p. 536.

39   *History of Kearny County, Kansas*, Vo. 1 p. 359

40   *History of Kearny County, Kansas*, Vol. 1, p.358

41   Blanchard, *Conquest of Southwest Kansas*, p. 255

42   Blanchard, *Conquest of Southwest Kansas*, p. 121

43   Blanchard, *Conquest of Southwest Kansas*, p. 121-122

44   *The Garden City Irrigator*, May 17, 1883

45   Blanchard, *Conquest of Southwest, Kansas* p. 125

46   The Kansas Historical Society has a tattered copy of this lithograph in its collections. Entitled the *Kansas Banner* it shows a goateed Jones carrying the banner with the rooster on top. The border of the print is surrounded by Kansas corn. The text of the banner beneath the picture read as follows. "The Banner That Boosted Blaine and Locked the Logan Link. This is a copy of the large Banner that was carried through the streets of Chicago on the evening of June 5th, 1884 by the Kansas Delegation to the National Republican Convention, followed by an enthusiastic Blaine multitude and headed by the best band of Chicago playing 'Hail Columbia' and other patriotic airs. Again, a critical moment, when Blaine's chances hung in the balance [on the motion to adjourn] this Banner was carried through the Convention Hall with the Rooster perched on top of it and card board in its mouth as above, which

created the wildest excitement, and aroused great enthusiasm for the "Plumed Knight." Upon the announcement of Blaine's nomination this victorious Banner was again carried through the aisles of the Convention Hall with the portrait of John A. Logan attached, which foreshadowed the final result, Blaine and Logan. Standard Bearer was C.J. Jones, Alternate Garden City, Kansas; Copyrighted by C.J. Jones, Alternate Garden City Kansas.

47 *Finney Country Directory, 1886-1887*, p. 57-59

48 *Finney County Directory, 1886-1887*, p. 61-62

49 Blanchard, *Conquest of Southwest Kansas*, p. 306

50 Paul Schullery, "Buffalo Jones and the Bison Herd in Yellowstone: Another Look," *Montana: The Magazine of Western History*, Vol. XXVi, No. 3, July 1976, p. 49. The scout, Peter Holt, was to receive half of all of the profits generated by this invention until he had received $1000 then he would receive 10 % of the profits.

51 *Garden City Herald*, May 26, 1888 Finney County Historical Society Clipping File

52 Gary Lee Kraisinger, *"Historical Notes on the Garden City Nickel Plate Railway, C.J. "Buffalo" Jones' Dirt Railroad,"* M.A. Thesis, Kansas State Teachers College, p. 21-22.

Chapter 4 : BUFFALO JONES AND THE PRESERVATION OF THE AMERICAN BISON

53 Inman, *Buffalo Jones*, p. 37. It would be of interest to know to whom he sold these buffalo and for what purpose.

54 Kersey, *Buffalo Jones*, p. 51.

55 Inman, *Buffalo Jones*, pp. 47-48.

56 Inman, *Buffalo Jones*, p. 48.

57 Inman, *Buffalo Jones*, p. 49-50

58 Inman, *Buffalo Jones*, p. 50.

59 Inman, *Buffalo Jones*, p. 51.

60 Inman, *Buffalo Jones*, p. 56.

61 Inman, *Buffalo Jones*, p. 80.

62 Inman, *Buffalo Jones*, p. 81. Inman, Buffalo Jones, p. 82 claims that a white catalo was killed on the Smokey Hill River in western Kansas and that its preserved and mounted hide was given to the State Agricultural Museum in Topeka.

63 Hough's account, "A Buffalo Hunt Indeed," is included in Inman's *Buffalo Jones*, p. 111-166. Hough became not only the author of numerous pieces of western fiction but also an advocate for the preservation of western wildlife. He worked diligently to see that the bison in Yellowstone were not eliminated through poaching and unlimited hunting.

64 Inman, *Buffalo Jones*, p. 112.

65 *Garden City Herald, September 29, 1887* in Buffalo Jones Clipping File, Finney County Historical Society.

66 The details of Jones' life are often obscure. How, why, and when he moved from Garden City, Kansas to McCook, Nebraska and how and where he obtained the buffalo that he had in McCook is not stated. If he drove his small herd from Garden City, then that in itself would be an epic adventure. Inman in presenting these events merely notes that he presents this information form extracts in Jones' diary, Inman, *Buffalo Jones*, p. 225.

67 The *Runic* has a fascinating history built in 1889 for the White Star Line was designed to carry a 1000 head of live cattle from the United States to Great Britain and cargo on its western voyage. After being sold several times she was renamed the *Imo* and became a whaler in the South Pacific. On December 6, 1917, she collided with the French munitions carrier *Mont Blanc* in Halifax harbor, Nova Scotia. Within twenty minutes, the *Mont Blanc* exploded killing more the 3600 inhabitants of the Richmond section of the city, 9000 were injured and property losses were estimated to be more than $35,000,000. Paradoxically, the *Imo* escaped with minimal damage and was again renamed. As the *Guvernoren*, she ran aground in the Falklands in 1920 and was completely lost.

68 Inman, *Buffalo Jones*, p. 228.

69 Inman, *Buffalo Jones*, p. 229.

70 Inman, *Buffalo Jones*, p. 236.

71 Inman, *Buffalo Jones*, p. 237.

72 Inman, *Buffalo Jones*, p. 242.

73 Jones comments on the pasturing and fencing of buffalo may be found in Inman, *Buffalo Jones*, pp. 246-258.

74 Inman, *Buffalo Jones*, p. 263.

75 Inman, *Buffalo Jones*, p. 264.

76 Buffalo Jones Clippings in the Kansas Scrapbook/Biography J/ Vol. 1/ Ja-Ju/323-338/ in the Kansas Historical Society.

77 Buffalo Jones Clippings in Biography File 4, Kansas Historical Society.

78 United States Department of the Interior National Park Service, "History of the Bison in Yellowstone Park," Chief Ranger's Office, File No. 715-03. Copy in Buffalo Jones Papers, Finney County Historical Society, Garden City, Kansas.

79 Aubrey L. Haines. *The Yellowstone Story, A History Of Our First National Park.* (Yellowstone National Park: Yellowstone Library and Museum Association in cooperation with Colorado Associated University Press, 1977), p. 395.

80 Easton and Brown, *Lord of Beasts*, pp.263-263 present evidence which they believe supports Roosevelt's appointment of Jones as Game Warden.

81 Since he was at the park in August of 1902, there seems to be little evidence for the story that Jones drove a herd of buffalo from Kansas to Yellowstone that summer and fall.

82 The bears were becoming a problem in the park because the private hotel and camp managers used the bears to attract tourists. At one period in the park's

history, stands were erected for visitors to sit on near the hotel garbage dumps.

83   Finney County, *History of Finney County, Kansas*, Vol. 1, p. 122

84   Paul Schullery presents a more critical review of Jones' actions in Yellowstone in his "Buffalo Jones and the Bison Herd in Yellowstone: Another Look," *Montana: The Magazine of Western History*, Vo. XXVI, No. 3, July, 1976, pp. 40-52.

85   Easton and Brown, *Lord of Beasts*, p. 134.

86   Easton and Brown, *Lord of Beasts*, p. 140-141.

Chapter 5 : PURSUIT OF THE MUSK OX

87   Inman's examination of Jones' attempts to capture the musk oxen is the most lengthy section in his *Buffalo Jones' Forty Years of Adventure* and reveals how knowledgeable Jones was about life in the Far North. In these passages, one learns of how familiar Jones was with Arctic exploration, the geography and peoples of these high latitudes, and how experienced he becomes in Arctic travel and survival. Inman devotes eleven chapters to Jones experiences in the North.

88   Inman, *Forty Years of Adventure*, p. 287.

89   Inman, *Forty Years of Adventure*, p. 308

90   In Canada, aboriginal people or referred to as the First People.

91   Inman, *Forty Years of Adventure*, p. 373

92   Inman, *Forty Years of Adventure*, p.384-386

93   Inman, *Forty Years of Adventure*, p. 388

94   Inman, *Forty Years of Adventure*, pp. 392-393

95   Inman, *Forty Years of Adventure*, p. 401.

96   Inman, *Forty Years of Adventure*, p. 403.

Chapter 6 : ZANE GREY AND BUFFALO JONES: THE CREATION OF A WESTERN AUTHOR

97   Zane Grey scholars cannot identify precisely when and where this meeting took place. Even one of Grey's most diligent scholars, Stephen J. May, cannot provide certainty on this question. See May's *Zane Grey's Romancing the West* (Athens: Ohio University Press, 1997), p.48-49 and May's Maverick Heart, *The Further Adventures of Zane Grey* (Athens: Ohio University Press, 2000), p. 47. Frank Gruber offers an undocumented but plausible account of their meeting in his *Zane Grey* (New York: A Signet Book from New American Library, 1971), pp. 69-70.

98   Gruber, *Zane Grey*, p. 69-70; May, *Romancing the West*, p. 49-50

99   Undated typescript of letter from Zane Grey, Altadena, California in Buffalo Jones Files, Finney County Historical Society

Chapter 7 : THE AFRICAN EXPEDITIONS OF BUFFALO JONES

100   May, *Maverick Heart*, p. 53, quoting Grey.

101   For a succinct review of his African experiences, please see James B. Wolf's "Buffalo Jones and the Conquest of the East African Frontier," *Journal of American Culture*, Fall, 1986, Vol. 9, pp. 39-48.

102   Guy H. Scull, *Lassoing Wild Animals in Africa* (New York: Frederick A. Stokes Company, 1911), p. xi-xiii

103   Henry Jay Case, *Guy Hamilton Scull* (New York: Duffield & Company, 1922) p. 175

104   Guy Scull is a fascinating figure. He fought not only with the Rough Riders in Cuba, but he had also been a traveler and correspondent to South Africa during the Boer War, Venezuela, the Balkans, and Manchuria. He had been a cowboy, Rough Rider, and cavalry man.

105   Case, *Guy Hamilton Scull*, p.177

106   Case, *Guy Hamilton Scull*, p. 178

107 Scull, *Lassoing Wild Animals in Africa*, p. 52

108 Case, *Guy Hamilton Scull*, p. 182.

109 Easton and Brown, *Lord of Beasts*, p. 196.

110 Scull, *Lassoing Wild Animals in Africa*, p. vi. Roosevelt's trip to East Africa

111 Easton and Brown, *Lord of Beasts*, p. 202, quoting *The Kansas City Star*, March 22, 1914. The costs of this expedition were substantial, but its major funding sources are unknown. It has been suggested by contemporary source that a circus company may have provided support. The daughter of Ambrose Means stated that it was believed that Jones was to receive $250,000 to bring back a live, adult, male gorilla. This gorilla was to be used in an experiment to see if it would breed with human females. There is no extant evidence to support such a proposition. See Easton and Brown, *Lord of Beasts*, p. 272 for more discussion of this theme.

Chapter 8 : THE END OF LIFE

112 *U.S. Patent Office Official Gazette*, August 29, 1916, p. 1514, Patent # 1,96,696 Water Elevator, Charles J. Jones, Portales, New Mexico, "Filed March 24, 1915".

ROTARY CLUB OF GARDEN CITY, KANSAS

The Rotary Club was the first "service club" in Garden City. George Finnup, a prominent Garden City businessman, had visited the Dodge City, Kansas Rotary Club and was impressed with the fellowship and activities of the group. He returned to Garden City and discussed the idea with Judge William Easton Hutchison. The Garden City Rotary Club was established by the Dodge City Rotary Club on December 26, 1922 and was admitted to Rotary International on January 9, 1923.

Judge Hutchison served as the first president. He and the following nineteen well-known community leaders composed the charter membership:

John E. Baker	Warren A. Maltbie
J. Ralph Bosworth	Chester M. McAllister
Benjamin Bullard	E. Lester McCoy
Walter O. Carter	Charles Rewerts
Chester H. Cleaver	Everett W. Ross
Frank D. Conard	Charles I. Vinsonhaler
Floyd H. Couchman	Theodore P. Wadley
Frank A. Gillespie	John F. Walters
William R. Haage	Charles I. Zirkle
Hubert O. Judd	

ROTARY CLUB INTERNATIONAL

Rotary was the world's first "service club" and was formed in 1905 in Chicago, Illinois. The name "Rotary" was derived from the early practice of rotating meetings among members' offices. Reaching out to improve the lives of the less fortunate has been the firm resolve of every Rotary Club.

In 1985, Rotary made an historic commitment to immunize all of the world's children against polio. Hundreds of thousands of volunteers were mobilized worldwide; and, by the 2005 target date, Rotarians will have contributed half a billion dollars to the cause.

Today, Rotary has over 1.2 million men and women who belong to 31,000 clubs in 166 countries. All are dedicated to the Rotary Club motto, "Service Above Self".

The tradition of "Service Above Self" continues. In 2004-2005, the Garden City, Kansas Rotary Club funded the publication of this book, designating it as a Rotary Club International Centennial project.